Natural Resources Governance and Sustainable Livelihoods in Uganda

Adonis & Abbey Publishers Ltd

St James House
13 Kensington Square,
London, W8 5HD
United Kingdom

Website: http://www.adonis-abbey.com
E-mail Address: editor@adonis-abbey.com

Nigeria:
Suites C4 – C6 J-Plus Plaza
Asokoro, Abuja, Nigeria
Tel: +234 (0) 7058078841/08052035034

Copyright 2019 © ACODE

British Library Cataloguing-in-Publication Data
A catalogue record for this book is available from the British Library

ISBN: 978-1-906704-36-0

The moral right of the author has been asserted

All rights reserved. No part of this book may be reproduced, stored in a retrieval system or transmitted at any time or by any means without the prior permission of the publisher

Natural Resources Governance and Sustainable Livelihoods in Uganda

Edited by

Onesmus Mugyenyi, Ronald Naluwairo & Russell Rhoads

Acknowledgement

The Editors gratefully acknowledge the assistance that has made this book volume possible. We are grateful for support from the development partners who supported the research that produced the book chapters. In a special way, we would like to acknowledge the financial support from DANIDA through CARE Denmark in partnership with CARE International in Uganda and the Democratic Governance Facility (DGF) contributing partners: The Netherlands, Norway, Sweden, Ireland, Austrian Development Cooperation, United Kingdom (UK), and the European Union (EU). DFID through Practical Action (Lima) also supported the research on local content which appears as one of the book chapters.

We are also appreciative to the Think Tank Initiative (TTI) which provided core funding to ACODE that made it possible to explore a wide range of issues on governance within Uganda while at the same time making the staff and research associates committed to scholarship.

Special thanks go to Professor David Francis and Professor Kenneth Omeje who until recently were based at the Bradford University's John and Elnora Ferguson Centre for African Studies (JEFCAS) for their technical and professional assistance in preparing this volume for publication. Profound debt is owed to the ACODE technical team who worked in concert with the Bradford team to prepare and transform this volume into a publishable form.

Table of Contents

Acknowledgement..iv
Table of Contents..v
Notes on Contributors..vi
List of Figures..xi
List of Tables..xii
Abbreviations..xii

Chapter One
Linking Natural Resources Governance and Sustainable Livelihoods
Ronald Naluwairo, Russell Rhoads, Onesmus Mugyenyi
....13

Chapter Two: Access to Justice in Uganda's Forestry Sector
Ronald Naluwairo and Anna Amumpiire
....27

Chapter Three: Local Content and Expanding Local Participation in the Oil and Gas Sub-Sector in Uganda
Elijah Dickens Mushemeza & John Okiira
....51

Chapter Four: Resolving Petroleum Conflicts in Uganda's Albertine Graben
Sebastiano Rwengabo
....73

Chapter Five: Land Acquisition and Resettlement: Safeguarding Community Livelihoods in Uganda
Russell Rhoads and Onesmus Mugyenyi
....99

Chapter Six: Fish Product Chain: The Case of Lake George in Uganda
Wilson Winstons Muhwezi and Boaz Blackie Keizire
....125

Chapter Seven: Management of National Oil Companies: Lessons For Uganda *Dan Ngabirano*

....157

Chapter Eight: Conclusion
Ronald Naluwairo and Onesmus Mugyenyi

....189

Index

....195

Notes on Contributors

Onesmus Mugyenyi is a Research Fellow and Deputy Executive Director at the Advocates Coalition for Development and Environment (ACODE). He has previously served as a Lecturer at the National College of Business Studies, Nakawa, Makerere University Business School and Makerere University, Kampala. He holds a Master of Laws degree majoring in International Economic Law and Environmental Policy from Makerere University. He also holds a post-Graduate Diploma in Legal Practice from Law Development Centre. He is an Advocate of the High Court of Uganda. He has extensive experience in policy research and has published widely on issues of environment and natural resource governance.

Russel Rhoads is a Socio-cultural Anthropologist, with Master's and PhD from the University of Kentucky, USA. He is an Associate Professor of Anthropology, Grand Valley State University (Michigan, USA) and a Research Associate at ACODE. He is trained in applied anthropology with a specialty in agricultural development, forced displacement and resettlement, globalization, policy research, and ethnography/qualitative research. His research interests explore the intersection between local food and global systems. He has conducted fieldwork in Mexico, Venezuela, Sierra Leone, and Uganda. His recent scholarship focuses on development-induced displacement, resettlement and community engagement. Rhoads was a Fulbright Scholar (2014-2015) at Makerere University, Kampala, Uganda.

Ronald Naluwairo is a Senior Research Fellow at the Advocates Coalition for Development and Environment (ACODE) and Senior Lecturer at the School of Law, Makerere University. He holds a PhD from the University of London, LL.M from the University of Cambridge, LL.B (Hons) from Makerere University and a Diploma in Legal Practice from Law Development Centre. He has extensive experience working on issues of natural resources governance and human rights. He is a well published scholar on these issues.

Anna Amumpiire is a Research Officer at Advocates Coalition for Development and Environment (ACODE). She has an LLM in Environmental Law and Policy from the University of Kent, Canterbury United Kingdom, a Bachelor of Laws Degree (LLB) from Makerere University, a Post-Graduate Diploma in Legal Practice from the Law Development Centre and is enrolled as an advocate of the courts of Judicature in Uganda. Her areas of interests are in environment and natural resources governance.

Elijah Dickens Mushemeza is an academic, and author. He is a Professor of Political Science and Development Studies at Ankole Western University and a Senior Consultant at Advocates Coalition for Development and Environment. Previously he worked as Dean Faculty of Business and Development Studies at Bishop Stuart University. He holds BA, in Social Sciences, an MA degree in Development Studies and a PhD degree in Political Science from Makerere University. He is also a consultant on Education, Governance, Poverty, Politics, Conflict, Forced Migration, Security, Oil and Gas, and Development issues generally in Africa. He has also previously worked as a Coordinator of the MA degree programme in International Relations and Diplomatic Studies in the Department of Political Science and Public Administration, Makerere University. He has taught at Mbarara University of Science and Technology. Professor Mushemeza is a past alternate Executive Committee member of the Council for the Development of Social Science Research in Africa.

John Okiira is a Research Officer at Advocates Coalition for Development and Environment (ACODE). He is an Economist by profession with a Master's degree in Social Protection Financing (Distinction) under the auspices of International Development Research

Centre (IDRC) from University of Mauritius. He also holds a Bachelor of Arts degree in Economics from Makerere University. John also has more than six years of experience in research and analysis obtained from various assignments at ACODE, Policy Analysis and Developmental Research Institute (PADRI), Uganda National Council of Science and Technology (UNCST) and African Institute for Strategic Research, Governance and Development (AISRGD). John's areas of interest are Economic Growth and Development, Governance and Service Delivery, Management of Natural Resources, Poverty and Social Protection.

Sabastiano Rwengabo is a Research Fellow at the Advocates Coalition for Development and Environment (ACODE), where he researches on the Governance of Oil and Gas Wealth in Uganda and East Africa. A Uganda- and Singapore-trained Political Scientist, Rwengabo holds a Doctor of Philosophy (PhD) degree from the National University of Singapore (NUS). He was a President's Graduate Fellow at NUS where he taught undergraduate courses in International Relations, International Security, and Civil Military Relations, before re-joining the Social Sciences community in Africa in 2015. Rwengabo has research interests and publication record on Civil - Military Relations, International Politics/Security, Regionalism and regional security measures under the African Union (AU), Urban Security, Democratization, Nation Building, and Governance of Strategic Resources.

Boaz Blackie Keizire is the Head of Policy and Advocacy at the Alliance for a Green Revolution in Africa (AGRA). He was formally a Head of Division of Agriculture and Food Security and Team Leader of a Pan-African Agricultural Reform Programme, the Comprehensive Africa Agriculture Development Programme (CAADP) at the African Union Commission (AUC) in Addis Ababa, Ethiopia. Earlier, Boaz was a Senior Advisor on CAADP at the AUC and headed Agriculture and Natural Resource Planning at the National Planning Authority in Uganda. He previously was a Principal Economist and a CAADP Lead Person in Uganda. He is also a Research Associate with Advocates Coalition for Development and Environment (ACODE). His areas of expertise are: Agricultural Economics, Agriculture and Natural Resource Policy Development, Analysis and Planning. He holds a Master's Degree in Agricultural Economics from Makerere University, Uganda and a

Postgraduate Diploma in Policy and Planning from the United Nations University, Reykjavik, Iceland.

Wilson Winstons Muhwezi is a Director of Research at Advocates Coalition for Development and Environment (ACODE) and an Associate Professor in Behavioural Sciences and Mental Health at Makerere University College of Health Sciences. He has a PhD (Medical Science) jointly conferred by Karolisnka Medical University, Stockholm, Sweden and Makerere University, Kampala. He has a Master of Philosophy Degree (Health Promotion) from University of Bergen, Norway and a Bachelor's Degree in Social Work and Social Administration from Makerere University. He has over 20 years' experience in basic and applied research analysis and advocacy. He is experienced in psychosocial work, community-based research as well as monitoring and evaluation. He has mentored students at Makerere University and Uganda Christian University. The uniqueness of his experience arises from his involvement with matters that straddle social sciences and health sciences. He has authored over forty scholarly articles and got them published in international peer reviewed journals. He has written several policy papers and policy briefs on topical issues, text book chapters and many consultancy reports. He is result oriented, highly analytical and self-motivated. He is comfortable to work in multi-disciplinary teams.

Dan Ngabirano is a Partner at Development Law Associates and an Assistant Lecturer in the Environmental Law Department at the School of Law, Makerere University. Presently, he is a Fulbright Scholar and SJD Candidate at the University of Iowa in the US. He holds a Bachelor of Laws Degree (LLB) from Makerere University and a Master of Laws Degree (LLM) from Harvard University, USA. Over the years, he has published, advised and consulted for a number of regional and international bodies, non-profits and private clients on diverse areas of law and policy, including natural resources law, environmental law, revenue law and taxation. Dan is also a member of The Access Initiative (TAI) and the Access to Information Committee of the African Network of Constitutional Lawyers (ANCL) international and regional initiatives seeking to promote transparency and accountability in the natural resources sector.

List of Abbreviations

ACODE	Advocates Coalition for Development and Environment
AGM	Annual General Meeting
AIA	Access to Information Act
AIDS	Acquired Immune Deficiency Syndrome
BHP	Bujagali Hydroelectric Power
BMUs	Beach Management Units
BNOC	British National Oil Company
CAO	Chief Administrative Officer
CBOs	Community-Based Organizations
CCA	Commodity Chain Analysis
CEO	Chief Executive Officer
CSOs	Civil Society Organizations
DFO	District Forest Officer
DFR	Department of Fisheries Resources
DRC	Democratic Republic of Congo
EITI	Extractive Industries Transparency Initiative
FSSD	Forest Sector Support Department
GDP	Gross Domestic Product
GNP	Gross National Product
GNPC	Ghana National Petroleum Company
GoU	Government of Uganda
HIV	Human immunodeficiency virus
IFCs	International Finance Corporations
IPIECA	International Petroleum Industry Environmental and Conservation Association
IOCs	International Oil Companies
JLOS	Justice and Law Reform Sector
JVP	Joint Venture Partner
LCs	Local Councils
LCMCs	Local Content Monitoring Committees
LCPs	Local Content Policies
LGs	Local Governments
MANRUIA	Matiri Natural Resource Users and Income Enhancement Association
MEMD	Ministry of Energy and Mineral Development
MPE	Ministry of Petroleum and Energy
NCDMB	Nigeria Content Development and Monitoring Board

NFA	National Forestry Authority
NGOs	Non-Governmental Organizations
NNPC	Nigeria National Petroleum Corporation
NOCs	National Oil Companies
NOGP	National Oil and Gas Policy
NPD	Norwegian Petroleum Directorate
NWP	Nature Wealth and Power
OPEC	Oil Producing and Exporting Countries
PAPs	Project Affected Persons
PFM	Participatory Forest Management
POCs	Private Oil Companies
PPP	Public-Private Partnerships
PROMINP	Programme for the Mobilization of the Oil and Gas Industry
QEPA	Queen Elizabeth Protected Area
RAPs	Resettlement Action Plans
RBP	Regulatory Best Practice
TAI	The Access Initiative
TAT	Tax Appeals Tribunal
UIA	Uganda Investment Authority
UHRC	Uganda Human Rights Commission
UNCITRAL	United Nations Commission on International Trade Law
UNDP	United Nations Development Programme
UPDF	Ugandan People's Defense Forces
US	United States
USA	United States of America
USAID	United States Aid for International Development
USD	United States Dollar
UWA	Uganda Wildlife Authority

CHAPTER ONE

Linking Natural Resources Governance and Sustainable Livelihoods

Ronald Naluwairo, Russell Rhoads and Onesmus Mugyenyi

Uganda, like most developing countries in the Sub-Saharan Africa, is endowed with valuable natural resources - minerals, fisheries, forests, fresh water bodies and rivers, good climate, vast arable land and natural touristic attractions, including wildlife. These resources contribute significantly to the livelihoods of the Ugandan population. The mining sector has potential to contribute significantly to the national development and already provides employment to thousands of artisanal miners; the agriculture sector employs approximately 69 per cent of the population and contributes over 26 per cent of the annual GDP (Uganda Bureau of Statistics, 2014; Republic of Uganda, 2015). The nation currently holds 50 per cent of the available arable land in East/Sub-Saharan Africa. Forestry provides 90 per cent of the energy needs of the country and is a source of livelihood to many people. The tourism sector is currently among the fastest-growing sub-sectors and accounts for 9.9 per cent of GDP.

The discovery of commercially viable oil and gas in 2006 added to the excitement expressed by most analysts regarding the country's potential to leap into the middle income country status in less than a decade. The oil and gas sub-sector is now expected to be the most crucial contributor to Uganda's economic and social transformation. In 2016, the government granted operating licences to Total E&P Uganda and Tullow Oil Uganda Plc (Though Tullow sold part of its interest to China's CNOOC later) and production is expected to begin in 2023. The estimated 1.7 billion barrels of oil that lies across 3 major fields in the country in the Albertine Graben is expected to be a game changer in the national revenues mix.

However, governance of these resources still remains a major challenge. Weak resource governance has led to unprecedented loss and degradation of the country's natural resources. In the forest sector for instance, Uganda's forest cover has been reduced from 4.9 million hectares in 1990 to 1.8 million hectares in 2015 (Republic of Uganda, 2016). This translates into a loss of 3.1 million hectares (Republic of Uganda, 2016). The arable land is shrinking significantly due to poor farming methods and climate change impacts, and fish catches have declined, leading to closure of some of the fish processing industries. All this is happening at a time when Uganda's population growth rate remains astonishingly high. According to the National Housing and Population Census Report 2014, Uganda's population in 2014 stood at 34.6 million, representing an increase of 10.4 million persons from 2002 (Uganda Bureau of Statistics, 2016). The unsustainable use of the country's natural resources amidst a rapidly raising population threatens the livelihood security of many people in Uganda.

This book describes research and evidence-based studies that contribute to an understanding of natural resource governance and its impact on sustainable livelihoods of the population. It builds on the existing knowledge about twin themes of natural resource governance and the impact on local communities to foster sustainable livelihoods. The individual case studies cited in the chapters apply to several sectors: forestry , oil and gas, and fisheries among others. The central argument in this book is that good natural resource governance is critical if the majority of the people in Uganda are to achieve positive outcomes in poverty reduction, balanced with development and economic growth. Consequently, the positioning of natural resource governance on livelihoods cuts across all the book chapters.

Conceptualizing Natural Resource Governance and Sustainable Livelihoods

Natural resource governance consists of the norms, institutions and processes that determine how power and responsibilities over natural resources are exercised, how decisions are taken, and how citizens – women, men, indigenous peoples and local communities – participate in and benefit from the management of natural resources (IUCN, Springer, 2016).

Good governance is important for ensuring sustainable management of the natural resources, and it also determines the extent to which the natural resources can be harnessed to improve livelihoods. Good resource governance is underpinned by six key principles: accountability, transparency, participation, effectiveness, efficiency, fairness and equity. By ensuring these principles, revenues generated from exploitation of the natural resources are guaranteed. It also guarantees that potentially exploitable natural resources like oil and public forests are used not for personal benefits but to better the livelihood of the majority.

Literature on natural resource governance has been accumulating over the recent past. Such literature ranges from describing paradigms of policy to implementation processes and other specific programmes (Murphree and Martin, 2016). Recent literature on the key dynamics of resource governance in Africa has addressed issues of security (Samadi and Mirabbassi, 2017), poverty reduction (Abdulai and Shamshiry, 2014), sustainability (Munang and Andrews, 2014), tourism (Christie et al., 2014), and land acquisition, displacement and resettlement (Cernea and Mathur, 2008). The key themes in the literature are sector-specific and relevant to the diversity of the African context, linking development to "good fit" policy, practical solutions and land management (Owusu et al., 2014).

Many of these issues are integrated into the chapters in this volume. It is argued that the lessons learnt from the case studies are applicable elsewhere. Applicability is even more noticeable when one attempts to analyse natural resource governance. Certainly, interrogating the issue of the meaning of "good governance" and gaps in legislation require robust frameworks that draw on international best practices, such as local content and benefit sharing. Secondly, the role of local governance and civil society cannot be minimised. The impact of decentralization and civil society on development, service delivery and the implementation of intervention programmes to save natural resources are underscored.

Sustainable Livelihoods

How is natural resource governance connected to livelihoods? The word "livelihood" as used in this book includes "the capabilities, assets and activities required for a means of living" (Chambers and Conway, 1992). In other words, livelihood is the totality of abilities, resources and the different ways through which people make a living, including natural assets, human capital, social capital, physical capital and financial capital (Kollmair and Gamper, 2002). This conceptualisation conforms to that used by the International Finance Corporation (IFC), in which the term "livelihood" refers to the full range of means that individuals, families, and communities utilize to make a living, such as wage-based income, agriculture, fishing, foraging, other natural resource-based livelihoods, petty trade, and bartering (International Finance Corporation 2012).

In the context of globalization, several pressing issues are raised (Hilson, 2016). The chapters in this volume ask key questions about the impact of governance and accompanying programmes on local community livelihoods, and when livelihoods can be considered sustainable. As Kollmair and Juli rightly put it:

> A livelihood can be classified as sustainable, when it is resilient in the face of external shocks and stresses, when it is not dependent upon external support, when it is able to maintain the long-term productivity of natural resources and when it does not undermine the livelihood options of others (Sneddon, 2000; Kollmair and Gamper, 2002).

Each chapter addresses livelihood impacts tied to practice and implementation, local participation, property rights, economic and social benefits, local resilience, and the sustainable management of natural and human resources. While a significant body of literature has emerged recently on the connection between resource management and sustainable livelihoods, the chapters in this volume offer a reconsideration of conceptualisations such as how communities are positioned as engines of development in resource management schemes (Massoud *et al.*, 2016). Such a debate is ongoing on how the participation of the local communities fosters conservation in the context of promoting development – where the outcomes of ecological sustainability can collide with the demands of local communities to control their own natural resources (Kopnina, 2012).

Three additional areas of investigation affecting livelihoods are noteworthy in this volume local content, benefit sharing and livelihood restoration caused by dislocation. In terms of local content, local content policies promote indigenous/community participation in sectors geared for the extraction of raw materials, such as minerals and petroleum. They encourage the development of local products and service provision using backward/forward linkages along the value chain (Ovadia, 2016). In this volume, benefit sharing is connected to forest management and the literature advocating for institutional change to reduce inefficiencies and corruption, as well as to help communities better manage forest resources while contributing to market growth (International Finance Corporation, 2015).

Finally, Khatun *et al* view benefits-sharing programmes (especially REDD+) as an attempt to adapt existing forms of forest governance to the needs of forest conservation and to the quest for land-use emission reductions, stating that:

> This approach to the climate problem runs the risk of repackaging landscapes as carbon sinks, and in doing so it can change how these landscapes are represented. . . what they are valued for, and what are the legitimate land-management objectives, rights and responsibilities . . Such transformations in the valuation of landscapes can transform motivations for conservation, and bring additional investments to local communities; but we need to be aware that they can also impose additional burdens, especially for those who are most often excluded from participation and benefit sharing in forest management and conservation efforts (Khatun *et al.*, 2015).

This transformation of landscapes challenges scholars and practitioners to pay close attention to social and cultural changes (as well as the economic) and land conflicts arising from forest governance restructuring and benefit sharing (John and Kabote, 2017).

Policy/Legal Framework Challenge and Gaps

Each of the chapters begins with an in-depth analysis of policy frameworks in order to determine the challenges and gaps that undermine policy implementation. This is essential as a way to mitigate the general weakening of sector policies. This weakening reflects a trend towards "softer" approaches to regulation to accommodate a more pro-business agenda and to speed up resource development (Khoday and Perch, 2012). One bright spot is the renewal of the "Natural Resource Charter," which establishes a set of principles to guide governments' use of natural resources, so that economic opportunities result in maximum and sustained returns for a country's citizens (Natural Resource Governance Institute, 2014). The Charter is based on 12 core precepts offering guidance on key decisions governments face, beginning with whether to extract resources and ending with how generated revenue can produce maximum good for citizens. All the links in this chain need to be strong if a country is to truly benefit from the management and extraction of resource wealth.

We identify a major need for a legislative shift where policies and priorities should be put into place that reflects the unique national contexts. For example, with respect to land acquisition and resettlement, a study by Tagliarino assessed the laws of 50 countries against indicators from the 2012 Voluntary Guidelines on the Responsible Governance of Tenure of Land (VGGT) (Tagliarino, 2017). The study found that more than half the countries did not have legal provisions for fair compensation that meet international standards. While Uganda fared better than most, the author recommends that robust compensation procedures established by law, coupled with respect for the rule of law, can help ensure that expropriations promote sustainable development outcomes that balance property rights with public interest.

Clearly, there is room for policy reform to integrate more inclusive, sustainable growth models. The chapters in this volume echo the policy attention to social responsibility, augmenting the roles played local government and civil society:

> Legal and regulatory regimes focused on natural resources need to adapt tocalls for social accountability. In particular, a need exists to reset the checks andbalances between government, the private sector and civil society, expand accessto judicial remedies, support maintenance of ecosystem services, means foraccountability and transparency to citizens, equity in land rights and tenureand implementation, and enhanced oversight mechanisms (Khoday and Perch, 2012:13).

As demonstrated elsewhere in Africa, decentralization in Uganda provides space and opportunity to link policy frameworks to local communities though local governance and civil society, in ways that promote democracy (Haruna and Kannae, 2016). It is important to note that in every country in Africa there is some form of local government in operation (Ribot, 2003). Today, the objective of nearly all of local government reforms is towards decentralisation in order to strengthen democratic governance, service provision, and the local governance of natural resources. The chapters here contribute to the literature that identifies direct roles for local government and civil society in resource governance for local populations (Olowu and Wunsch, 2004).

For example, in the emerging petro-state in Uganda, a study by Van Alstine highlights the emerging spaces for civil society, but finds significant governance gaps: lack of coherence among civil society organisations (CSOs, NGOs, CBOs); limited civil society access to communities and the deliberate centralisation of governance; industry driven interaction at the local level; and weak local government capacity (Van Alstine *et al.*, 2014). In addition, another line of inquiry and debate can investigate how the representatives of donors, states, and non-governmental organizations create and assert "moral" narratives, specifically tied to the human/animal/conservation interaction sphere.

Organization of the Chapters

The chapters in this volume focus on forests, fisheries, land, and oil and gas. The book interrogates selected governance issues raised above and offers a critical perspective for the sustainable management of these resources and livelihoods. One of the biggest governance issues in the management of Uganda's natural resources is the question of access to justice. Good natural resource governance and livelihood security of the resource-dependent and adjacent communities require a robust system of access to justice. Inadequate or lack of access to justice undermines resource governance and threatens the livelihoods of the resource-dependent communities. Chapter 2 chronicles issues synthesized qualitatively in assessing access to justice in the forestry sector. It is established that while there have been attempts at improvement, access to justice in Uganda's forest sector is still generally weak. The authors identify several gaps both in law and practice with respect to access to forest information; tenure rights of forest adjacent communities; liability for forestry harm; and redress mechanisms for forest disputes. Unless and until these gaps are adequately addressed, efforts undertaken to improve forest governance and community livelihoods are more likely to register dismal success.

Chapter 3 focuses on local content and expanding local participation in the oil and gas sector in Uganda. Since the discovery of commercially viable oil deposits in 2006, one of the big debatable issues is how Ugandan citizens can effectively participate and benefit from the oil and gas industry. This question is important because there are diverse experiences where the exploitation of oil and gas never benefited the citizenry in any appreciable detail. The authors focus on policy and other measures which countries like Uganda can employ to prepare their citizens to effectively participate and benefit from the oil and gas exploitation. The chapter explores the meaning of local content and local participation and how best countries like Uganda should develop and implement regulatory frameworks to ensure maximum benefits for the citizens. The authors identify bottlenecks to local participation in Uganda and provide policy actions that the Government of Uganda and other actors can take to ensure that Ugandan citizens effectively participate and benefit from the oil and gas industry.

It is also argued that effective local participation and benefit from the oil and gas industry can be determined by deliberate government policies, strategies, legislations, contracts and actions that enhance the capacity of its citizens to take advantage of the opportunities presented by the industry. Countries that adopt local content frameworks with clear and entrenched provisions on local content are more likely to register better outcomes in terms of skills developed, participation of local companies and generation of jobs for citizens. The authors, however, caution that adoption and implementation of frameworks on local content and local participation must go hand in hand with well-functioning implementation institutions such as national oil companies, enterprise centres, and monitoring and measuring Boards. Although the authors recognise Uganda's draft local content policy as progressive, they call for increased awareness and ownership of this policy once it is adopted and published. To guarantee effective participation, they also call for the enactment of an enabling legislation and detailed contracts that commit companies involved in the sector to implement local content provisions that enhance local participation, economic diversification and livelihoods.

With the discovery and exploitation of oil in Uganda, many scholars have predicted escalation of new conflicts not only within Uganda, but also between Uganda and its neighbouring states. Oil-related conflicts threaten to undermine the potential of harnessing Uganda's oil resources for national development and improved livelihoods. For Uganda's oil resources to have meaningful and lasting impact on livelihoods and development, establishment of appropriate and effective redress mechanisms is a must. Chapter 4 analyses the mechanisms for resolving intra-state and cross-border conflicts and examines their applicability to potential oil conflicts in the Albertine Graben. The author assesses the Albertine Graben's conflict proneness by underscoring existing and potential conflicts. By examining the nexus between oil and gas wealth and intra-state and inter-state/cross-border conflicts, the author analyses the ways through which these conflicts are resolved. It is established that existing conflict resolution mechanisms are neither coordinated nor adapted to oil conflicts. The author proposes ways of developing and adapting new multilevel conflict-resolution mechanisms to oil conflicts. It is contended that effective resolution of oil conflicts requires the development, operationalisation, and coordination of multilevel conflict-resolution mechanisms at intra-state, bilateral, and regional-international levels. It is further argued that instituting prior conflict management measures makes it easy for state and non-state actors to predict, detect, mitigate, de-escalate, and resolve oil conflicts.

As demand for land for Government infrastructural projects and investments increases, land expropriation becomes a common phenomenon in Uganda and is projected to increase rapidly with the development of the petroleum sector. Land expropriation often leads to displacement of people resulting in loss of agricultural land and businesses, and other sources of livelihood. The challenge thus is how to ensure that land taking minimises or does not negatively affect the livelihood security of project affected persons. In Chapter 5, Rhoads and Mugyenyi interrogate this question. They analyse the triggers for land expropriation in Uganda and using case studies, they examine the impacts of land expropriation on community livelihoods. They expose a disconnect between the legal and policy protection of the rights of individuals to land and livelihood on one hand, and the actual realization of the rights in the course of implementing government development projects on the other hand. They conclude that the existing policy and implementation for land acquisition in Uganda is uneven and inadequate for safeguarding the rights of project affected persons. They call for an approach that "balances development" – accounting for the needs of citizens, national development priorities and the needs of developers and industry. To this end, the authors recommend the formulation of a comprehensive policy on land acquisition and resettlement including development of a robust action plan that provides checks and balances to mitigate negative consequences on livelihoods. They also recommend that mechanisms for engaging communities during the project planning and implementation (e.g. fair compensation, valuation of property, sensitization, monitoring, and grievance procedures) must be integrated into policy frameworks.

In Chapter 6, using the case of Lake George, Muhwezi and Keizire analyse investigate why Uganda's fishing communities remain poor, in spite of having access to wealth in the fishery resource. The chapter describes the main actors in the fish production and marketing chain, determines the income gains and/or losses that accrue to different actors in the fish production chain and proposes appropriate responses. It is argued that the behaviour patterns among actors in the fish product chain largely account for the marginal economic gains they make. The authors consequently argue that interventions should take cognisance of the nature, power and wealth relations over any resource, as well as behavioural characteristics of main actors. If not, attempted intervevtions will most likely make dismal impact in terms of poverty reduction and improved livelihoods. They recommend supporting the fisher-folk to diversify into other economic activities like rice-growing so as to relieve the lakes of current fishing pressure, introduction of 'closed seasons' (periods of no fishing) so as to allow the lake to regenerate, and conflict resolution mechanisms.

The discovery of commercially viable oil and gas resources in Uganda has created great expectation among the citizenry about the livelihood opportunities and revenue it will generate for personal and national growth and development. To realize maximum benefits from these resources, Government established the National Oil Company (Natoil) to ensure proper management of these resources. However, for Natoil to achieve the expected outcomes, it must be properly governed and managed in accordance with internationally recognized standards and best practices. In Chapter 7, the author explores a number of international standards and best practices from which he draws lessons for the proper management of Natoil.

The final chapter of the book appraises the lessons learnt from the case studies and offers a clearer understanding of resource governance and how it impacts on community livelihoods. Uganda serves as a laboratory for experimentation, reflecting accelerated development and economic changes at the local, regional and national levels. The implications of the Ugandan case, we emphasize, are instructional for countries and regions elsewhere during this era of uneven globalization in Africa. Most importantly, development dynamics impact people on the ground. It is hoped that the lessons and the recommendations stemming from this research will be seriously considered by policy makers and other stakeholders to enhance the governance of Uganda's natural resources for better and sustainable livelihoods of the people.

References

Abdulai, A. M. and Shamshiry, E. (2014) 'Theory and Practice on the Nexus Between Poverty, Natural Resources and Governance', in *Linking Sustainable Livelihoods to Natural Resources and Governance*. Springer Singapore, pp. 11–40.

Cernea, M. M. and Mathur, H. M. (2008) *Can Compensation Prevent Impoverishment? Reforming Resettlement through Investments and Benefit-Sharing*. New Delhi, India: Oxford University Press.

Chambers, R. and Conway, G. R. (1992) *Sustainable Rural Livelihoods: Practical Concepts for the 21st Century*. Cambridge.

Christie, I., Christie, I. T., Fernandes, E., Messerli, H. and Twining-Ward, L. (2014) *Tourism in Africa: Harnessing Tourism For Growth And Improved Livelihoods*. World Bank Publications.

Haruna, P. F. and Kannae, L. A. (2016) 'Implementing Good Governance Reform in Ghana: Issues and Experiences with Local Governance', in *Public Administration in Africa: Performance and Challenges*.

Hilson, G. (2016) *Natural Resource Extraction and Indigenous Livelihoods: Development Challenges in an Era of Globalization*. Routledge.

International Finance Corporation (2012) 'IFC Sustainability Framework', *Policy and Performance Standards on Environmental and Social Sustainability*, (Performance Standard No. 5). Available at: http://www.ifc.org/wps/wcm/connect/topics_ext_content/ifc_ext ernal_corporate_site/ifc+sustainability/our+approach/risk+manage ment/performance+standards/environmental+and+social+perform ance+standards+and+guidance+notes

International Finance Corporation (2015) *The Art and Science of Benefit Sharing in the Natural Resource Sector*. Washington, DC: International Finance Corporation.

IUCN (no date) *Natural Resource Governance Framework: A Knowledge Basket of the International Union for Conservation of Nature*. Available at: https://www.iucn.org/sites/dev/files/content/documents/nrgf_up

date.pdf (Accessed: 10 June 2017).

John, P. and Kabote, S. J. (2017) 'Land Governance and Conflict Management in Tanzania: Institutional Capacity and Policy-Legal Framework Challenges', *American Journal of Rural Development*, 5(2), pp. 46–54.

Khatun, K., Gross Camp, N., Corbera, E., Martin, A., Ball, S. M. J. and Masso, G. (2015) 'Participatory Forest Management In Kilwa District, Tanzania: Insights On Governance, Benefit Sharing And Implications For REDD+', *Environment and Planning A*, 47, pp. 10–2112. Available at:https://doi.org/10.1177/%0A0308518X1559589.

Khoday, K. and Perch, L. (2012) *Development From Below: Social Accountability in Natural Resource Management*. International Policy Centre for Inclusive Growth.

Kollmair, M. and Gamper, J. (2002) 'Input Paper for the Integrated Training Course of NCCR North-South Aeschiried', *Development Study Group*. University of Zurich, pp. 5–7.

Kopnina, H. (2012) 'Toward Conservational Anthropology: Addressing Anthropocentric Bias in Anthropology', *Dialectical Anthropology*, 36(1–2), pp. 127–146.

Massoud, M. A., Issa, S., El-Fadel, M. and Jamali, I. (2016) 'Sustainable Livelihood Approach Towards Enhanced Management of Rural Resources', *International Journal of Sustainable Society*, 8(1), p. 54 72.

Munang, R. and Andrews, J. (2014) 'The Next Steps: Africa's Sustainable Development Goals and Their Implications', *Environment: Science and Policy for Sustainable Development*, 56(5), pp. 4–11.

Murphree, M. and Rowan, M. (2016) 'Shifting Paradigms, Policy and Processes in Conservation and Development Over the Past Four Decades. Social Science Research Network (SSRN), Rochester, New York. Available at: https://ssrn.com/abstract=2840612 or http://dx.doi.org/10.2139/ssrn.2840612

Natural Resource Governance Institute (2014) *Natural Resource Charter*. 2nd edn. Available at: https://resourcegovernance.org/analysis-tools/publications/natural-resource-charter-2nd-ed.

Olowu, D. and Wunsch, J. S. (2004) *Local Governance in Africa: The Challenges Of Democratic Decentralisation*. Boulder and London: Lynne Rienner.

Ovadia, J. S. (2016) 'Local Content Policies and Petro-Development in Sub-Saharan Africa: A Comparative Analysis', *Resources Policy*, 49, pp. 20–30.

Owusu, F., D'Alessandro, C. and Hanson, K. T. (2014) 'Moving Africa Beyond the Resource Curse: Defining the "Good-Fit" Approach Imperative in Natural Resource Management and Identifying the Capacity Needs', in *Managing Africa's Natural Resources*. Palgrave Macmillan UK.

Republic of Uganda (2015) *Second National Development Plan 2015/6 – 2019/2020*.

Republic of Uganda (2016) *State of Uganda's Forestery 2016, Ministry of Water and Environment*. Kampala: para.

Ribot, J. C. (2003) 'Democratic Decentralisation of Natural Resources: Institutional Choice and Discretionary Power Transfers In Sub-Saharan Africa', *Public Administration and Development*, 23, pp. 53–65.

Samadi, M. and Mirabbassi, S. B. (2017) 'Realization of Human Security in Light of Good Governance', *J. Pol. & L*, 10, p. 84. Available at: http://www.ccsenet.org/journal/index.php/jpl/article/download/65431/35356.

Sneddon, C. S. (2000) 'Sustainability in Ecological Economics, Ecology and Livelihoods: A Review', *Progress in Human Geography*, 24(4), pp. 5210–5549.

Springer, J. (2016) Initial Design Document for a Natural Resource Governance Framework. NRGF Working Paper No. 1. Gland, Switzerland: IUCN and CEESP.

Tagliarino, N. K. (2017) 'The Status of National Legal Frameworks for Valuing Compensation for Expropriated Land: An Analysis of Whether National Laws in 50 Countries/Regions across Asia, Africa, and Latin America Comply with International Standards on Compensation Valuation', *Land*, 6, p. 2.

Uganda Bureau of Statistics (2014) *Uganda National Household Survey 2012/2013*. Kampala.

Uganda Bureau of Statistics (2016) 'The National Population and Housing Census of 2014: Main Report'.

Van Alstine, J., Manyindo, J., Smith, L., Dixon, J. and AmanigaRuhanga, I. (2014) 'Resource Governance Dynamics: The Challenge Of "New Oil" In Uganda', *Resources Policy*. Elsevier, 40(June), pp. 48–58. Available at: https://doi.org/10.1016/j.resourpol.2014.01.002.

CHAPTER TWO

Access to Justice in Uganda's Forestry Sector

Ronald Naluwairo and Anna Amumpiire

Introduction

Although the last one and half decades have witnessed a vibrant national discourse on environmental governance, little attention is given to issues of access to environmental justice in general, and access to justice in the forestry sector in particular. Access to environmental justice is internationally recognised as key in ensuring sustainable management of natural resources and promoting environmental democracy (United Nations, 1992). It is also important for improving the livelihoods of the natural resource dependent communities.

Using qualitative data, this chapter analyses the state of access to justice in Uganda's forestry sector. Most of the analysis in the chapter is based on work earlier published in ACODE research series. The analysis focuses on only three aspects of access to justice i.e., access to information in the forestry sector, the protection and enjoyment of tenure rights of forest adjacent communities and liability for forestry harm. In this connection, the chapter assesses: the adequacy of the law and practice in guaranteeing access to information in Uganda's forestry sector; the adequacy of the law and practice with respect to the protection and enjoyment of tenure rights of public forests adjacent communities; and the adequacy of the law and practice relating to liability for forestry harm. Using three court cases, the chapter also provides some lessons for enhancing the role of courts as forest dispute settlement mechanisms.

The chapter is organised in seven parts. In Part 2, the Chapter analyses the concept of access to justice and its relevance to Uganda's forestry sector. In Part 3, the chapter analyses the law and practice with respect to access to information in the forestry sector. Part 4 is concerned with the recognition and protection of tenure rights of Uganda's forest adjacent communities. In Part 5, issues of liability for forestry harm are examined. Through the lens of three decided court cases, Part 6 provides some lessons for enhancing the role of courts in promoting forest justice. In Part 7, the Chapter ends with some concluding observations about the state of access to justice in Uganda's forestry sector and what needs to be done to improve it. Before addressing the specific objectives of this study, it is important to first briefly explore the concept of access to justice and why it is important for Uganda's forestry sector.

Access to Justice and Its Relevance for Uganda's Forestry Sector

Access to justice in the forestry sector derives from the concept of 'access to environmental justice'. Together with the access rights to environmental information and participation in decision-making concerning environmental matters, access to environmental justice is internationally recognised as key in ensuring environmental democracy and sustainable development (Pring and Pring, 2009). But what does 'access to justice' mean? And what does it mean in the context of forest governance? Why is access to justice in the forestry sector important for a country like Uganda?

The United Nations Development Programme (UNDP) aptly summarised the meaning of the concept of 'access to justice' from the human rights perspective as '… the ability of people to seek and obtain a remedy through formal or informal institutions of justice, and in conformity with human rights standards' (UNDP, 2005). The Access Initiative (TAI) ('Implementation of Principle 10 of the Rio Declaration of the United Nations Conference on Environment and Development', 2013), defines 'access to environmental justice' as "the ability of citizens to turn to impartial and independent arbiters to resolve disputes over access to information and participation in decisions that affect the environment, or to correct environment harm". From these definitions, access to justice in the forestry sector as a derivative from environmental justice can be defined as the ability of citizens or other legal persons to seek and obtain a remedy from impartial and independent arbiters over disputes concerning: access to forest information; participation in decision making processes that affect the use and management of forests; and harm/destruction occasioned or likely to be caused to forests.

Access to justice in the forestry sector is principally concerned with four major issues: citizens and other legal persons being able to challenge decisions that deny them access to information in the hands of public authorities concerning the use and management of forests; ensuring public participation in decision-making concerning the use and management of forests; preventing and or remedying harm caused to forests; and effective enforcement of environmental laws and policies that ensure the conservation and sustainable use of forest resources.

Access to justice is important for forest governance for a number of reasons. First, it facilitates citizens' inclusion and participation in decision-making processes regarding forest management (Pring and Pring, 2009). Second, it is important for protecting the rights and guaranteeing the livelihood security of the forest adjacent communities. The ability to access justice enables the poor and vulnerable communities and other persons to protect their rights against infringement by other persons and entities. Third, access to justice in the forestry sector is essential in holding relevant government agencies, private individuals, companies and other duty bearers accountable in as far as the management and utilisation of the forest resources is concerned. Fourth, through access to justice, the environment and natural resources can be protected further as it facilitates the citizenry and other persons to seek redress and remedy for forestry harm (Foti *et al.*, 2008). It is for these among other reasons that analysis of access to justice in Uganda's forestry sector is important. What then is the state of access to justice in Uganda's forestry sector and what issues need to be addressed? These among other questions are the focus of the next section.

Access to Information in Uganda's Forestry Sector

Effective access to justice in the forestry sector requires adequate legal guarantees to ensure public access to information regarding forests in possession of forest-mandated public bodies. Besides promoting transparency and accountability, access to information is very important in empowering the citizenry to not only to participate in the management of their country's forest resources but also in enforcing their rights as far as these resources are concerned (Foti *et al.*, 2008).

There are a number qualitative elements internationally used to assess adequacy of forest legal frameworks in ensuring access to information. A robust forest legal framework should not only explicitly provide for the right of access to information but should also provide clear procedures for requesting and accessing information in possession of public forest bodies (Davis *et al.*, 2013). It should also define the type of forest information that should be made publicly available, and in case confidential information, should explain why such information is kept confidential. Additionally, the law should also provide a timeframe within which requests for information should be responded to. Fees and other legally prescribed requirements associated with accessing information in possession of the public forest bodies should be reasonable and affordable. It is also important that the law provides for the right of appeal in case one is not satisfied with the response from the public forest body in respect of his/her request for information. The question to ask now is – Against these indicators, how adequate is Uganda's legal framework in ensuring access to information in the possession of the public forest mandated agencies?

Read together with the Access to Information Act 2005 (AIA), Uganda's forest specific legislation is strong with respect to issues of access to information. The major challenges are with the practice/implementation. The National Forestry and Tree Planting Act 2003 (herein after referred to as 'the Forestry Act'), explicitly provides for the right of access to information. In no uncertain terms, Section 91 (1) provides that, 'every citizen has a right of access to any information relating to the implementation of this Act, submitted to or in the possession of the State, a local council, the Authority or a responsible body'.

Although the Forestry Act restricts the right of access to only information in respect of its implementation, the AIA which governs issues of access to information in the possession of Government and all public bodies generally allows for access to all information in possession of public bodies. It provides that:

> Every citizen has a right of access to information and records in possession of the state or any public body except where the release of the information is likely to prejudice the security or sovereignty of the state or interfere with the right of privacy of any other person.

It is clear that the right of access to information provided for in Uganda's forest legislation is not restricted to information in possession of the State authored by the State or its agencies. It suffices that the information sought regardless of its origin or authorship is in possession of the State, its organs or agencies. This is important for access to justice because public can access a lot more information than it would if the right was to be restricted to only information authored by the State and its agencies.

Commendably, for every public body, the AIA designates a specific office to be responsible for issues of access to information. It places the responsibility of ensuring that the records of a public body are accessible on the Chief Executive Officer of that body. In Uganda's forestry sector, this means that the Commissioner Forest Sector Support Department (FSSD) and the Executive Director of the National Forestry Authority (NFA) are the responsible persons. To facilitate access to information further, the AIA requires information officers of public bodies to prepare a manual of functions and index of records. In terms of the procedure to access information, Section 91 (2) of the Forestry Act provides that a person desiring information from a public body shall apply to that body and shall be granted access to the information on the payment of prescribed fees, if any in a prescribed manner. Read in conjunction with Section 10 of the AIA, the application for access to forest information should be made to the Chief Executive Officer of the relevant public forest bodies. Section 11 of the AIA provides the details that must be included in the application for access to information. Section 16 of the AIA requires that the information officer to whom a request for access is made should within 21 days after the request notify the person requesting access to information of the decision. With a manual of functions and index of records in place, 21 days is a reasonable time frame, also considering the fact that the reason for the information requested may be time-bound.

Aside from the broad exceptions to the right of access to information provided in Part III of the AIA, two major weaknesses of Uganda's forest legislation with respect to the issue of access to information are worth highlighting. First, although the law explicitly provides for the right of access to information, it does not provide for any offence in respect of public officials who deny applicants information requested for without any lawful excuse. Section 46 of the

AIA which would be applicable only deals with a person who: a) destroys, damages or alters a record; (b) conceals a record; or (c) falsifies a record or makes a false record, with intention to deny the right of access to information. It does not cover cases of outright denial of the right of access to information without legal justification. Given the potential impunity with which some public officers may act, making it criminal to deny public access to information without lawful excuse would deter/reduce impunity. This is good for forest justice.

Second, in accordance with the Constitution of the Republic of Uganda and the AIA, Uganda's forest legislation restricts the right of access to forest information to only Ugandan citizens. The rationale for restricting the right of access to forest information to only Ugandan citizens is problematic from the perspective of the broader objective of that right - which is to promote efficient, effective, transparent and accountable governance. Foreign nationals including regional and international organisations play important roles in promoting transparency and accountability in the forest sector. Within certain limitations, they should also enjoy the right of access to forest information. In a mini-survey carried out September and October 2016 by ACODE, out of 14 representatives of NGOs interviewed, 10 respondents did not think that the restriction of the right of access to forest information serves any useful purpose. Three out of four officials interviewed from FSSD and NFA also felt that the restriction was not necessary. The one official who insisted that the right of access to information should be restricted to citizens argued that the foreign nationals can always access the information they want through the citizens.

Although it can generally be concluded that Uganda's law is fairly strong, there are serious gaps and challenges in practice that affect the actual realisation of the right of access to information in Uganda's forest sector. First, both NFA and FSSD which are the principal public forest bodies do not have a manual of functions and index records to facilitate access to information as required by law. At NFA, each department has its own list of the information and records (Director of Corporate Affairs of NFA, personal communication). At FSSD, one of the officials interviewed acknowledged that while the Department has a lot of information, the lack of a manual of functions and index of records makes it difficult even for fellow staff to know what information is available and in whose custody it is (Senior Forest Officer, FSSD, personal communication). Second, a lot of information held by NFA and FSSD is incomplete and not up-to-date. For instance, with respect information about local forest reserves, one of the officials interviewed from FSSD admitted that they have very scanty information. He stated that while FSSD regularly sends templates to the local governments to get up-to-date information, most local government officials do not oblige '.... it is also not routine to get information from local governments. District Forest Officers do not respond to requests for information; they also do not have computers, some do not even know where the local forest reserves are so it creates a challenge of availability of and up-to-date information', he argued.

Third, some respondents complained of non-response and/or delay in responding to their requests for information and getting informal oral responses to their requests for information. Regarding the former, one of the respondents shared that after making endless follow-ups in vain, he had to 'sit at NFA almost the whole day' until he was given part of the information he wanted. Regarding the latter, two respondents complained about the difficulty of crosschecking the authenticity of information given by word of mouth and the challenge of relying on it and referring to it in research.

There are also a number of requests for information made to the public mandated forest bodies that are blatantly denied or ignored without any justifiable reason. Two examples will suffice to illustrate this point. In *Edward Ronald Sekyewa t/a HUB for Investigative Media v. National Forestry Authority*, the applicant's request for information regarding procurement of equipment for prohibiting, controlling and management of fires in 506 central forest reserves was ignored by the Executive Director of the Respondent. The major issue was whether the Respondent was lawfully justified to refuse the request for access to information sought by the applicant. At the hearing, counsel for the respondent argued that the applicant being a private entity ought to have disclosed the reason and purpose for which the information was required since there was a possibility of jeopardizing public interest in case the information was misused.

Relying on Section 6 of the Access to Information Act, His Worship Boniface Wamala rightly ruled that the reason for which the information is required and the belief of the officer supposed to provide the information as to the purpose for which the information is required are irrelevant considerations. He argued that whether the applicant had given any specific reasons or not, the application had to be considered on its merit. His Worship took strong exception to the fact that the Respondent never made response to the Applicant's request for information even when the applicant followed up his request after 5 months with a letter. "If the problem was non-disclosure of the purpose of information, the Respondent would have written back to the Applicant communicating so," argued His Worship Wamala.

In another case involving the same parties i.e., *Edward Ronald Sekyewa t/a HUB for Investigative Media v. National Forestry Authority*, on 2nd September 2013, the Applicant lodged with the Executive Director of the Respondent a request for access to information regarding the implementation and operationalization of Forestry Information System under Priority 8 of the Respondent's Business Plan 2009 -2014. The Executive Director of the Respondent failed and/or refused to give a decision on the Applicant's request within the statutory period of 21 days after receipt of the request form. The main issue was whether the Respondent was lawfully justified to refuse the request for access to the information sought by the Applicant. The respondent argued that after due considerations, they declined to grant the Applicant's request because the information requested for was available on the Organization's website and was accessible to the public and that the non-release of the information did not prejudice the Applicant. The Respondent never communicated its decision to the applicant in spite of his notice of reminder.

His Worship Boniface Wamala agreed with counsel for the applicant that the Applicant''s request was specific and precise. It was about the 'steps that had been taken to establish the forestry information system as indicated under Priority 8 of the Respondent's Business Plan (2009 - 2014) and confirmation of the operational status of the Forestry Information System Business Plan 2009-2014.'This information was not on the Respondent's website. What was on the website was the Respondent's Business Plan (2009-2014). Most important, His Worship held even if the information actually requested for was on the Organization's website, the Respondent was still duty bound to respond to the Applicant's request and deliver the information in one of the modes anticipated by the Access to Information Act. In the final analysis, His Worship Wamala ruled that by simply declining and keeping quiet upon receiving the Applicant's request, the Respondent was not in compliance with the clear provisions of the law. The Respondent was therefore not justified to refuse his request for access to the information sought.

These two cases summarised above point to the fact that even with a good law, there may be impediments to the actual realisation of the legally protected right of access to information. These can range from inadequate appreciation of the law and poor attitude among the duty bearers to the lack of adequate human and financial resources.

In sum, it can rightly be concluded that Uganda's forest legislation is fairly strong with respect to issues of access to information in the forestry sector. The actual realisation and enjoyment of the right of access to forest information is however affected by many factors including lack of manual functions and index of records by the forest-mandated agencies, lack of updated information on a number of issues, blatant denial of information by some public officers, inadequate appreciation of the law governing issues of access to information and the lack of adequate human and financial resources.

Protection and Enjoyment of Tenure Rights of Forest Adjacent Communities

One of the key areas for assessing the state of access to justice is the extent to which a country's legal framework recognizes and protects the tenure rights of forest adjacent communities. Forest tenure rights include ownership rights and secondary rights to access, use and manage forest resources. Under the extended bundle of rights, forest tenure rights include access rights, user rights (extraction rights), management rights, exclusion rights and alienation rights (Schlager and Ostrom, 1992; Larson et al., 2010; Larson and Dahal, 2012). Recognition and protection of tenure rights of forest communities is important not only because of role that forest adjacent communities play in conserving and managing of the forest resources but also because they suffer most from the negative effects of living near the forests. For instance, members of the local communities living near Matiri central forest reserve complain of vermin animals that destroy their crops and theft of their crops by illegal loggers. Justice therefore demands that tenure rights of these forest adjacent communities should be recognised and adequately protected. This protection is important as compensation for losses and inconveniences suffered; and also act as an incentive for the communities to sustainably manage the forest resources.

There are a number of qualitative elements internationally used to assess the adequacy of national legal frameworks in protecting and promoting tenure rights of forest adjacent communities. They include: scope of the tenure rights; duration of the rights; clarity and consistency of the rights; recognition of customary tenure rights; number and nature of restrictions on how the rights can be exercised/enjoyed; legal guarantees against unilateral extinction of the rights; and enforcement mechanism (FAO, 2011, 2012). Taking these factors into consideration, a critical analysis shows that Uganda's forest legislation is generally weak with respect to the protection of tenure rights of forest adjacent communities.

The only legally recognized and protected tenure right of forest adjacent communities is the right to dry wood or bamboo. This right is moreover provided for in a very ambiguous manner that makes its interpretation and application problematic. Section 33 (1) of the Forestry Act states that, subject to the management plan, a member of a local community may, in a forest reserve or community forest, cut and take free of any fee or charge, for personal domestic use in reasonable quantities, any dry wood or bamboo. This means that the only traditional use of forests which is indispensable to the local communities and which is compatible with the principle of sustainable development is the right to dry wood or bamboo. The law does not recognise and protect the customary tenure rights of forest communities beyond access to dry wood or bamboo.

What amounts to dry wood is not defined. The right to dry wood or bamboo is moreover subject to a number of limitations. First, going by the strict wording of Section 33 (1), at any one particular moment, a member of a forest community is entitled to either dry wood or bamboo and not both. Second, the dry wood or bamboo must be for personal domestic use. This means that one cannot take some dry wood or bamboo for their neighbour or ailing mother. Third, members of the forest communities are required to cut and take only reasonable quantities. What amounts to reasonable quantities and who determines it is not defined. Fourth, the right to cut and take dry wood or bamboo is not automatic. It is subject to the management plan of a forest reserve or community forest. This means that it is only acceptable where a forest management plan allows.

However, some stakeholders often argue that beyond the right to dead wood or bamboo, there are other rights that forest communities can have and enjoy under the Collaborative Forest Management (CFM) framework provided for under Section 15 of the Forestry Act. This is however not correct. Neither Section 15 of the Forestry Act, which provides for CFM nor the CFM Guidelines define any forest tenure rights for forest adjacent communities. What is not contestable however is that, under the CFM Framework, forest adjacent communities can enjoy some benefits from the forest reserves. Unlike rights which are legal entitlements, these benefits are not automatic. According to the CFM Guidelines, the benefits and roles of the different stakeholders under a CFM Arrangement are supposed to be negotiated and agreed upon in a CFM Agreement between and among the different stakeholders especially the forest user groups and NFA. Some members from Matiri central forest reserve adjacent communities formed a forest user group called *Matiri* Natural Resource Users and Income Enhancement Association (MANRUIA) and entered into a CFM Agreement with NFA. This CFM Agreement dated 9th February 2016 lists a number of benefits for the members of MANRUIA. These include: access to poles; access to forest foods like mushrooms and wild yams; access to craft materials like papyrus and palm leaves; access to dry dead wood; access to herbal medicine; fish farming and bee keeping.

A number of observations can be made about CFM arrangements as a source of forest benefits for the forest adjacent communities. First, under the current legal framework, it is only members of the forest adjacent communities who form themselves into forest user groups and enter into CFM Agreement with NFA who can access benefits. To-date, out of the 506 central forest reserves in Uganda, there are only 49 CFM Agreements in respect of only 20 central forest reserves. This means that beyond the right to deadwood or bamboo, majority of the communities living near Uganda's central forest reserves are not legally accessing any forest benefits. Second, benefits under the CFM Agreements are negotiated; the negotiations are largely between NFA and the representatives of the CFM group. This means that the benefits largely depend on the negotiation capacity of the representatives of the CFM groups. Third, there are a number of conditions placed on the enjoyment of the benefits. For instance, under the CFM Agreement between NFA and MANURIA, members can only access fuel wood (deadwood) twice a week on Tuesdays and Saturdays. Many respondents considered this an unnecessary restriction. It was argued for instance that the elderly depend on their grandchildren who go to school on Tuesdays to collect fuel wood which means that they would only have one day and fuel wood collected in one day is not enough to take them through the whole week. Forth, according to the Forest Regulations, CFM Agreements are entered into for an initial period of 5 years, which may subsequently be extended where the parties are in compliance with their obligations and where there is no objection by either party. Arguably, this means that the benefits lapse with the expiry of the Agreement. The fact that renewal is not automatic makes things worse.

In conclusion, Uganda's forest legislation is weak with respect to the protection of forest tenure rights of forest adjacent communities. In practice though, under the CFM arrangements, depending on their negotiation capacity, local communities or members of forest adjacent communities who form forest user groups and enter into CFM Agreement with NFA can access certain negotiated benefits from the central forest reserves. Accessing the benefits is subject to agreed conditions in the CFM Agreement and only happens during the subsistence of the Agreement. The benefits are also subject to the management plan of the respective forest reserve.

Liability for Forestry Harm

Effective access to justice in the forestry sector requires that the forest legal framework should have a comprehensive list of crimes in respect of harm or potential threats to forests. Additionally, the forest legal framework should prescribe strong and deterrent sentences for those who commit forest crimes and illegalities. The law should also not unnecessarily protect government officials when they make decisions that negatively cause harm or threaten the integrity of forests. Access to justice in the forestry sector also requires forest legislation to provide for some incentive/reward to members of the forest adjacent communities and other ordinary persons who aid in apprehending or successful prosecution of people involved in committing forest crimes and illegalities. These persons need to be rewarded for two major reasons. First, they put their lives and those of their families at risk. Second, the reward can act as incentive for many people who have information about persons committing forest crimes and illegalities to provide the information to the relevant authorities for action. This is good for forest justice.

With respect to the above areas of assessment, Uganda's forest legislation generally scores low marks. Although it contains a fairly comprehensive list of forest crimes, there are gaps that need to be addressed. For instance, compared to Kenya and Tanzania's forest legislation there are a number acts which are harmful or pose serious threats to Uganda's forests which constitute crimes in Kenya or Tanzania which are not criminalised in Uganda. For instance being found in possession of forest produce with respect to which an offence was committed; being or remaining in a forest reserve between limited hours; and aiding or abetting commission of certain forest crimes.

The penalties provided for in Uganda's forest legislation in respect of commission of forest crimes are also too weak. Most of the penalties are also not commensurate with the economic value of the crimes. As such, they are not helping much in deterring people from committing forest crimes and illegalities. One example will suffice to illustrate this point. According to Section 43 of the Forestry Act, a person found guilty of cutting, taking or removing forest produce from a forest reserve or community forest without a license is liable to a fine not exceeding thirty currency points or to imprisonment for a term not exceeding three years, or both. This means that even if one is found to have illegally cut trees worth billions of money, the maximum penalty one risks suffering is a fine not exceeding thirty currency points or imprisonment for a term not exceeding three years, or both.

Another weakness of Uganda's forest legislation with respect to penalties for forest crimes as is evident in the above provision is that it prescribes the maximum and not minimum sentence (ACCU, 2015). This is for instance unlike Kenya and Tanzania's forest legislation. The problem with Uganda's approach is that it gives a lot of discretion to the judicial officers in determining the final penalty to impose in a particular case. Evidence shows that they often give very lenient sentences notwithstanding the fact that the maximum sentences provided for are themselves weak. This is not good for forest justice.

Connected to the issue of penalties, there is growing evidence that where the offence committed attracts a fine or imprisonment or both, the magistrates normally go for the fines and not imprisonment. In cases where magistrates go for imprisonment, the sentences imposed are very short. As a result of the maximum fine that can be imposed being so low, many of the convicts do not find any challenges in paying the fines. In fact, one police officer stated that when attending court hearings, many suspects anticipate being fined if found guilty and often come with enough money to pay off the fine immediately.

Uganda's forest legislation is also weak with respect to the issue of rewards/incentives for informers. It does not provide for any reward to persons that help the authorities with information leading to the apprehension and/ or successful prosecution of people involved in committing forest crimes and illegalities. This is unlike forest legislation for countries like Tanzania. Section 99 (1) of the Tanzania's Forest Act– provides that 'The Director may award any amount not exceeding one half of any fine imposed for an offence against this Act to any person who may have supplied such information as may have led to the conviction of an offender'.

Redress Mechanisms: Lessons from the Matiri Court Cases for Enhancing the Role of Courts in Promoting Forest Justice

Effective access to justice requires existence of enough redress mechanisms at different levels with clear defined mandates to address forest disputes. The independence of the dispute resolution mechanisms should be guaranteed. The dispute resolution mechanisms should dispense justice in a timely manner and should offer effective remedies. In Uganda, courts of law remain the major mechanism for resolution of forest disputes. The way Ugandan courts dispense forest justice is increasingly becoming a matter of great concern to many stakeholders. Through an analysis of three cases concerning encroachment on *Matiri* central forest reserve, this section provides lessons for enhancing the role of courts in promoting forest justice. All the three cases involve the National Forest Authority (NFA) on one hand, and alleged encroachers on forest reserves on the other. These cases are: *Omuhereza Rwakaboyo & 119 others v The National Forestry Authority* (herein after referred to as 'Omuhereza 1); *Omuhereza Rwakaboyo & 119 others v The National Forestry Authority* (herein after referred to as 'Omuhereza 2'); and *Kalubanga Patrick and 40 others v National Forestry Authority* (herein after referred to as "the Kalubanga case'). Together, these three cases shall be referred to as "the *Matiri* court cases". These cases were chosen because Matiri central forest reserve is one of Uganda's major central forest reserves where there have been many forest disputes between local communities and NFA a number of which have ended into courts of law.

To guide the ensuing analysis, it is important to reproduce the facts of these cases in some detail. In *Omuhereza* 1, the plaintiffs claimed that they were owners of the suit land in *Matiri* central forest reserve. They claimed that they had stayed there over a long period of time and that they had developed the suit land in certain respects including construction of homesteads, establishing a trading centre, agricultural and mixed farming, and establishing ancestral and burial grounds. For some reasons, the plaintiff were opposed to the survey and reopening of the boundaries of *Mukonomura* enclave in *Matiri* central forest reserve and the fresh marking of internal and external boundaries of the central forest reserve. 0n 4th September 2009, they got an interim order of injunction restraining the defendant (NFA) from interfering with the suit land, alienating, gazetting, developing, controlling, managing or cultivating the suit land, planting trees or carrying out construction works or any other activity thereon, until the hearing and determination of the main application for a temporary injunction or until further orders from court. The interim order was confirmed by the judge who heard the main application and who subsequently granted a temporary injunction. The injunction was however to protect only the 'boundary of activities' as at 4/09/2009. For this purpose, the High Court ordered the District Forest Officer (DFO), District Agriculture officer (DAO), District Police Commander (DPC) together with a representative of the Chief Administrative Officer (CAO) Kyenjojo district to establish the 'boundary of activities' as at 4/09/2009. The High Court also ordered a survey and opening up of the boundaries within a specified period of time. The court orders were never executed. The plaintiffs continued with farming activities and cut more trees. NFA forest guards arrested and prosecuted some of the plaintiffs for illegal encroachment.

Both parties went back to court accusing each other of violating the court order. The plaintiffs denied any fresh encroachment and claimed that they were carrying out their activities within the lands where court allowed them to stay as at 4/09/2009. On 4th October 2013, the parties entered a consent order before the Assistant Registrar. According to this order, Kyenjojo district administration was again tasked to establish the 'boundary of activities' of the plaintiff as at 4/09/2009. Any activities beyond the interim order of 4/09/2009 would not stand protected and

NFA would act to recover any areas encroached upon. NFA claimed that the plaintiffs continued to cut down trees, harvest timber and burn charcoal and opened up new gardens in total breach of the consent order, a claim the defendants denied. On 6th October 2013, NFA filed a survey report with Court showing the recent update of true boundaries of *Mukonomura* enclave. The Plaintiffs rejected it.

Before making his ruling, Justice Batema visited the land in issue and noted a number of things among which was that the plaintiffs had adamantly rejected the findings of the government surveyor and instead showed him false boundaries based on colours painted on trees by forest study groups. The judge also noted that in the middle of *Matiri* central forest reserve is a private piece of *mailo* land known as *Mukonomura* enclave and that all encroachment on the forest arose out of absence of a clear boundary. It was further observed that the Court orders of injunction failed to maintain the status quo as at 4/09/2009. *Matiri* central reserve had been heavily encroached upon by the plaintiffs and other people and there were freshly opened gardens in the middle of the forest, and trees had been cut for timber and charcoal. Court also observed and noted that all houses and constructions in the suit land were temporary in nature.

In his ruling dated 25/07/2014, Justice Batema ordered for the lifting of all court orders of injunction and held that NFA was free to plant trees and protect and preserve the forest. All people who settled in lands outside *Mukonomura* enclave whether protected by the former court orders were given one month from the date of the ruling to harvest their crops and peacefully move out of the suit land. It was observed that their continued stay and cutting of the forest for timber and charcoal was causing irreparable damage to NFA and that court would have no forest to hand over to the NFA if it won the case. NFA was ordered not to interfere with the lawful stay and activities of the residents of *Mukonomura* enclave and the residents of *Mukonomura* enclave were ordered not to encroach on *Matiri* forest reserve as per the provisional boundaries established by the government surveyors in their report dated 6/10/2013. Although the one month's notice to vacate especially in respect of people who were protected by the former court orders may be considered inadequate, in the circumstances, it was the right decision to make if forest justice was to be achieved. The lessons for judicial officers from this ruling are discussed in the next section.

In *Omuhereza* 2, the plaintiffs appealed to the Court of Appeal against Justice Batema's ruling summarized above. They applied for a temporary injunction seeking to restrain the respondents (NFA), their agents or anybody claiming authority from them from entering and trespassing on the suit land until the determination of Civil Appeal No. 162 of 2014 which was said to be pending before the Court of Appeal. The grounds for the application were that there was a pending appeal which had overwhelming chance of success and that if the application was not granted, the appeal would be rendered nugatory and the applicants would suffer substantive and irreparable damage. That it was just and equitable to grant the application.

In his ruling dated 14th October 2014, Justice Kenneth Kakuru of the Court of Appeal first noted that the applicants' notice of appeal upon which the application was premised was lodged out of time according to the rules of court. Nevertheless 'taking into account the chequered history of this case, and the peculiar issues it raises' he was inclined to invoke the provisions of Rule 42(2) of the rules of the Court of Appeal to grant a consequential extension of time within which the notice of appeal ought to have been filed. He then proceeded to determine the application as if the notice of appeal had been lodged in time. Contrary to the applicants claim that they had filed Civil Appeal No 162 of 2014, Justice Kakuru found that there was no such appeal. Civil Appeal No.162 of 2014 was a different case altogether involving different parties.

Finding no merit in the application, Justice Kakuru dismissed it with costs. In dismissing it, he observed that the orders sought in the application were more or less the same as those the applicant intended to seek in the appeal itself, namely staying or setting aside the order of Justice Batema issued on 25th July 2014. 'I am hesitant to grant an order whose effect is to grant the relief sought in the intended appeal', he stated. He argued that granting such order would have the effect of reversing the decision of the High Court without hearing the parties on that decision.

According to the ruling, Justice Kakuru also found that the applicants did not establish that if their application was not granted they would suffer irreparable loss and damage. In fact, their counsel conceded that any loss or damage could be compensable by damages. He noted further that the applicants had not established that the intended appeal had any likelihood of success.

He found the balance of convenience to be in favour of the respondent. He argued that the applicants could be compensated for any damages or loss resulting from the order of the learned Judge but the damage to the Natural Forest reserve on the other hand would likely be irreparable and irreversible. As will be discussed in the next section, this ruling equally has important lessons for judicial officers in terms of enhancing their role in particular and courts of law in general in ensuring forest justice.

In Kalubanga, in November 2013, the applicants successfully applied for interim orders of injunction against NFA from evicting them. In this application, they applied for a declaratory order, an injunction to maintain the status quo and general damages and costs. They argued that unless and until the boundaries of the forest reserve were opened and ascertained, they ought not to be evicted on a mere presumption that they are occupying a forest reserve. Justice Batema who heard the application visited the *locus* and found among other things that *Mukonomura* enclave where the applicants claimed to leave was a private *mailo* land surrounded by Matiri central forest reserve. The judge found that the suit land was far away from the *Mukonomura* enclave and was in Matiri central forest reserve. He noted that unlike in *Omuhereza* 1, the applicants were not residents of *Mukonomura* enclave or immediate neighbours to the enclave. He further noted that they were clearly illegal encroachers who were degrading the forest and abusing court process. Against these observations, he dismissed the application with costs. In his ruling, he noted that the activities of the applicants were dangerous to the forest and were causing irreparable damage to NFA and all the citizens of Uganda. He directed NFA to ensure that all farming activities and the cutting of trees for timber and charcoal burning in the suit land were stopped henceforth.

The question to ask now is – What lessons do these cases offer to enhance the role of courts in promoting forest justice? The *Matiri* cases provide five important lessons for enhancing forest justice. First, resolving forest disputes in a timely manner is a must if courts are to be counted on as key partners in promoting forest justice and sustainable management of Uganda's forest resources. It took over five years for Court to dispose of *Omuhereza* 1. While it is appreciated that there might have been some factors beyond Court which could have contributed to the delay in concluding this case, given the forest destruction that can happen in just one day, five years is a very long time to spend in addressing forest disputes. Indeed, the delay in resolving this dispute resulted in unprecedented depletion of *Matiri* central forest reserve by the plaintiffs and others to the extent that as Justice Batema observed in his ruling, "[only] a small strip of the forest remains along the road side on the Kyenjojo-Kampala highway."

Second, in resolution of forest-encroachment related disputes, it is always important for judicial officers to visit the *locus in quo*. In both *Omuhereza* 1 and *Kalubanga*, the Judge visited the forest land in issue. The findings at the scene of the suit lands were very critical in enabling Court to reach informed and just decisions. In *Kalubanga* for instance, the judge stated the reasoning of his visit as thus:

> We chose to visit the locus in quo to see for ourselves the type of lawful settlement of the plaintiffs in the forest reserve. We did not want to listen to academic arguments and maintain a status quo of cutting trees and cultivating in a forest reserve which we thought was unlawful from the word go or gave no cause of action.

In this case, court noted a number of things that informed its decision. For instance, it found that the suit land was far away from the *Mukonomura* enclave (the private *mailo* land in the forest) and was in *Matiri* central forest reserve. Court also noted that unlike in the case of Omuhereza 1, the claimants in *Kalubanga* were not residents of *Mukonomura* enclave or immediate neighbours to the enclave. To this effect, court held that they were clearly illegal enrichers degrading the forest and abusing court process to get an injunction against NFA.

Third, another key lesson for judicial officers is that in applications for interim orders of injunctions, it should be borne in mind that often, NFA (as trustee of Uganda's central forest reserves) stands to suffer irreparable loss and damage if the applications are ruled against it. Consequently, even the balance of convenience should often be resolved in favour of NFA/ protecting the forests. Although cases differ, It is generally often much easier to compensate loss suffered by the alleged encroachers through damages than it is to NFA if the forests are destroyed. Thus, in *Omuhereza* 1, while ordering all people who settled in lands outside Mukonomura enclave to vacate the suit land, Justice Batema observed that it would be easier to hand back to them the forests if they won the main suit. Conversely, he noted that their continued stay and cutting of the forest for timber and charcoal was causing irreparable damage to NFA and that court would have no forest to hand over to the NFA if NFA won the case. In *Omuhereza* 2, while dismissing the application, Justice Kenneth Kakuru of the Court of Appeal found the balance of convenience to be in favour of NFA. He argued that the applicants could be compensated for damages or loss resulting from maintaining the ruling of the trial judge. On the other hand, he argued that the damage to the natural forest reserve was likely to be irreparable and irreversible.

Fourth, the *Matiri* court cases demonstrate the need for judicial activism in resolving forest disputes. Judicial activism requires judicial officers to go beyond merely applying the law to the facts. It requires them to innovatively make decisions and recommendations that advance forest justice. In *Omuhereza* 1, beyond just interpreting the law and applying the law to the facts and issues at hand, Justice Batema noted that having private *mailo* land located in a forest reserve was one of the challenges to ensuring the integrity of *Matiri* forest reserve. He observed that the enclave harbours criminal trespassers who encroach on the forest and carry out activities that endanger the forest. To save this forest, he recommended that the NFA should buy out the *Mukonomura* enclave so that all land becomes forest reserve. Given the history of encroachments on *Matiri* central forest reserve emanating from persons occupying *Mukonomura* enclave, there is no doubt that if implemented, Justice Batema's recommendation would go a long way in reducing cases of illegal encroachment and other forest crimes and illegalities in *Matiri* central forest reserve.

Finally, the *Matiri* cases teach us that where necessary, in the interest of saving forests, substantive justice should be done without undue regard to technicalities. Article 126 (2) (e) of the Constitution of the Republic of Uganda provides inter-alia that 'In adjudicating cases of both a civil and criminal nature…substantive justice shall be administered without undue regard to technicalities'. Although meeting technical requirements is an important part of the justice system, if upholding technicalities poses serious threats/harm to forests, judicial officers should follow the constitutional command to administer substantive justice without undue regard to technicalities. In *Omuhereza* 2, Justice Kenneth Kakuru could have dismissed the application as the applicants' notice of appeal was lodged out of time. But given the 'chequered history of this case, and the peculiar issues it raises' as he put it, he decided to grant a consequential extension of time within which the notice of appeal ought to have been granted. He consequently proceeded to determine the merits of the application which he found lacking in material respects.

Along with other interventions, including continuous training of judicial officers on issues pertinent to access to justice in the forestry sector, if taken-on, these lessons can go a long way in enhancing the role of courts in promoting forest justice and the sustainable management of Uganda's forest resources.

Conclusion

This Chapter was primarily concerned with analysing the state of access to justice in Uganda's forestry sector with respect to four major issues i.e., access to information in the forest sector, recognition and protection of tenure rights of forest adjacent communities, liability for forestry harm and redress mechanisms.

With respect to the issue of access to forest information, Uganda's forest law is generally strong. Read together with the AIA, Uganda's specific legislation not only explicitly provides for the right of access to information but also provides the general procedure for accessing information and timeframe within which requests for information must be responded to. It also explicitly provides for offices in public bodies charged with the responsibility of ensuring public access to information. Its major weakness is that it does not provide for any offence or punishment of public officials who blatantly refuse to respond to requests for information without any legal justifications and unnecessarily restricts the right of access to information to only Ugandan citizens. Despite the fairly strong legal framework, actual realisation and enjoyment of the right of access to information in the forest sector is affected by many factors. These include: lack of a manual of functions and index of records by the public forest bodies; general lack of up-to-date information by the public forest bodies; delays and non-response to requests for forest information; and at times blatant refusal by public officers to provide the requested information without any legal justification.

Concerning the protection and enjoyment of tenure rights of forest communities, Uganda's forest legislation is generally weak. The only legally recognised and protected right is the right to cut and take dry wood or bamboo for personal domestic use. This right is moreover provided for in a very ambiguous manner which cannot guarantee its effective enjoyment. Under CFM however, local communities and forest user groups who enter into CFM Agreements with the NFA can negotiate for and access some benefits from the respective central forest reserves.

Regarding liability for forest harm, Uganda's forest legislation is also generally weak. It is lacking in a number of respects. It does not criminalize certain acts which are harmful or pose threats to forests. The penalties provided for commission of forest crimes are also weak to deter forest crimes and illegalities. Uganda's forest law also gives a lot of discretion to judicial officers in determining the final sentences to impose once they convict someone for commission of a forest offence. Regrettably, Uganda's forest law does not also offer any rewards to members of the forest adjacent communities or other persons who assist law enforcement officers with information that can lead to successful apprehension or prosecution of people who commit forest crimes and illegalities.

With reference to redress mechanisms for handling forest disputes, Uganda's forest legislation does not establish any forest-specific redress mechanism nor does it provide for alternative dispute settlement. To enhance access to justice in the forestry sector, Uganda needs to improve its forest legislation to: introduce more forest crimes with respect to acts or omissions that may cause harm or threats to Uganda's forests; increase penalties for all forest crimes to among other things reflect the economic value of the offence; reduce the discretion of judicial officers in determining the final sentences to impose on convicts; and provide rewards to persons and forest adjacent communities that provide information which leads to successful apprehension and prosecution of persons who commit forest crimes and illegalities. Beyond the dry wood and bamboo, the law should also provide for more tenure rights for forest adjacent communities. Beyond the law, it is important that Uganda also addresses the non-legal challenges that affect issues of access to justice. For instance, in the context of access to information, there is need to invest in: creating a manual of functions and index of records of public forest-mandated agencies; getting up-to-date forest information; and training staff of public agencies on the law and other issues related to access to justice. To enhance the role of courts in promoting forest justice, there is need for timeliness, judicial activism and udue regard to technicalities in resolving forest-related disputes. In forest encroachment-related disputes, it is critical that judicial officers find time to always visit the locus in quo before giving judgment.

References

ACCU (2015) *When the Law Costs Conservation Efforts: A Critical Analysis into the Penalties under Uganda's National Forestry and Tree Planting Act 2003*.

Davis, C., Williams, L., Lupberger, S. and Daviet, F. (2013) *ASSESSING FOREST GOVERNANCE: The Governance of Forests Initiative Indicator Framework*. World Resources Institute.

FAO (2011) 'Framework for Assessing and Monitoring Forest Governance'. Rome: The Program on Forests.

FAO (2012) 'Voluntary Guidelines on Responsible Governance of Tenure of Land, Fisheries and Forests in the Context of National Food Security'. Rome.

Foti, J., de Silva, L., McGray, H., Shaffer, L., Talbot, J. and Werksman, J. (2008) *Voice and Choice: Opening the Door to Environmental Democracy*. Washington D.C.: The Access Initiative / World Resources Institute.

'Implementation of Principle 10 of the Rio Declaration of the United Nations Conference on Environment and Development' (2013) in *Caribbean Forum: Shaping a Sustainable Development Agenda to Address the Caribbean Reality in the Twenty-First Century*.

Larson, A. M., Barry, D. and Dahal, G. R. (2010) 'New rights for forest based communities: Understanding processes of forest tenure reform', *International Forestry Review*, 12(1), pp. 78–96.

Larson, A. M. and Dahal, G. R. (2012) 'Forest tenure reform: New resource rights for forest-based communities', *Conservation and Society*, 10(2), pp. 77–90.

Pring, G. and Pring, C. (2009) *Greening Justice: Creating and Improving Environmental Courts and Tribunals*. The Access Initiative.

Schlager, E. and Ostrom, E. (1992) 'Property rights regimes and natural resources: A conceptual analysis', *Land Economics*, 68(3), pp. 249–262.

UNDP (2005) *Programming for Justice: Access for All- A Practitioner's Guide to a Human Rights-Based Approach to Access to Justice*. Bangkok: UNDP Regional Office.

United Nations (1992) 'the Rio Declaration on Environment and Development', in *The United Nations Conference on Environment and Development*. Rio de Janeiro. Available at: www.unesco.org/education/pdf/Rio_E.Pdf%0a%0a.

CHAPTER THREE

Local Content and Expanding Local Participation in the Oil and Gas Sub-Sector in Uganda

Elijah Dickens Mushemeza and John Okiira

Introduction

Uganda has confirmed commercially viable oil and gas and first production is expected in 2023. Oil development activities have the potential to contribute to livelihood opportunities if well planned and governed. Many countries have devised various mechanisms to capture as much revenue as possible from their industries and create the conditions to expand the benefits from the oil and gas sub-sector to other economic sectors. "Local content" has gained popularity among policy makers as a strategy to achieve diversification and enhance the benefits from the oil and gas industry and create sustainable livelihoods (Easo and Wallace, 2014). Good local content frameworks can facilitate local participation, improve human and financial capital, and enhance the quality of natural capital-natural resources stock. Local content frameworks can also direct investment in physical capital which comprises of infrastructure and producer goods to support livelihoods and enhance social capital which are livelihood assets.

Since 2006, positive steps have been taken to develop the oil and gas resource for the benefit of the country. The National oil and gas policy (NOGP) was approved in 2008, the up-stream and mid-stream legislations were enacted in 2013 and the Public Finance Management Act was passed in 2015. The country is also in the final stages of developing the Local Content Policy intended to address issues of skills and work force development; and national industry participation. The big question that the citizens have continued to ask is how they will participate and benefit from the industry. This question is driven by experiences in many other countries where the resource has been discovered and exploited but has not benefited its citizens. The evidence from the literature reveals that effective local participation and benefit from the oil and gas industry is determined by deliberate government policies, strategies, legislations, contracts and actions that enhance the capacity of its citizens to take advantage of the opportunities presented by the industry.

This chapter unravels important actions required to prepare citizens to participate and benefit from the oil and gas exploitation. The evidence gathered and presented in this chapter is intended to inform the country to prepare citizens to participate the oil and gas sub-sector in a manner that will enhance wealth creation and sustainable livelihoods. The analysis has three main objectives: First, to explore the experiences of other oil and gas producing countries on local content and local participation. Second, is to identify the bottlenecks to local participation; and thirdly to identify actions required by government and other actors that can enhance Ugandans to participate and benefit from the oil and gas industry.

Understanding the Twin Concepts of Local Content and Local Participation

Local content can be defined as the extent to which the output of the extractive industry sector generates further benefits to the economy beyond the direct contribution of its value-added, as through links to other sectors (Tordo and Anouti, 2013). These links are created when the oil and gas industry, because of its operations, purchases inputs that are supplied domestically instead of importing them. In this sense, local content seeks to expand the share of nationally produced goods and services that are needed for oil and gas exploration, development, and extraction (Heum *et al.*, 2011). The aim of a local content policy is to expand the benefits beyond revenues of oil and gas activities for the national economy through the achievement of certain outcomes.

The most common outcomes that local content policies seek to address are local employment, skills development and national industry participation (Esteves *et al.*, 2013). Local employment and national industry participation are promoted when companies related to the oil and gas sector are required to hire national workforce and to purchase goods and services from national companies for the development of its operations. On the other hand, skills development is incentivized due to the fact that, to comply with the previous requirements, companies and government have to build skills and capacities in the national industry that provides goods and services as well as in the national workforce.

Local content policies aim to increase participation of the national industry, create job opportunities for nationals, and increase the level of local skills and capabilities. However, these policies can have downsides if they are not adapted to specific national contexts, including: slow procurement, higher industrial concentration in the extractive sector, hindering of production targets and competitiveness. They can also foster corruption and lack of transparency, more bureaucracy, among others (Tordo and Anouti, 2013). If policy to enhance local content is badly implemented or enforced, it may do worse to the economic development of the host country. Even if the policy is well developed, policymakers have to be aware that there are extra costs associated with local content expansion that can only be justified if they turn out to serve as investments that pay off in the future (Heum *et al.*, 2011).

Additionally, the implementation of local content policies can produce negative effects when increasing the participation of the local industry such as consuming wealth rather that creating value, attracting high cost investors and inferior industry development (Heum *et al.*, 2011). Furthermore, there are social impacts like demographic change associated with in-migration, concentration of economic activity around the project area, changes in patterns of land use, and institutional change (Esteves *et al.*, 2013).

Local Participation on the other hand means citizens are actively engaged through policy formulation, law making and implementation of the activities that benefit them. This is possible through their representatives (legislature), organized groups such as civil society organisations, private sector groups (enterprise centres, manufacturers associations, Chamber of Commerce), educational institutions that impart skills and competencies, business engagements such as supplies, procurement and employment (job creation and placement). This means there is a long chain of activities and processes in which citizens can scale up their participation. This is why it is important for countries of East African Community that are still improving their local content frameworks with limited outcomes in terms of employment, skills development and national industry participation must have deliberate policy actions that engage various categories of citizens in the oil and gas sector. The starting point is having well developed local content frameworks (policies, legislations, and contracts) through a participatory process, put in place institutions and mechanisms that allow a transparent participation, monitoring and evaluation, and appropriate documentation. The national institutions should be able to put in place measurement mechanisms on the progress made on the local content outcomes (Mushemeza and Okiira, 2016b).

Relevance of Local content to sustainable livelihoods

Several countries involved in oil and gas development have the desire to achieve sustainability of resource-led economic development and expansion of livelihood opportunities for citizens. This imperative has made these countries to adopt local content frameworks. Investment of rents, royalties and taxes from resource extraction is often seen as the only facet of development through natural resources. However, local content policies represent an important second avenue for achieving positive developmental outcomes from these resources (Ovadia, 2014). It is now established from the literature that local content encourages the employment of locals by multinational companies (MNCs), but also recognizes the resource extraction-particularly oil and gas-is an enclave industry that will never be a significant employer in its own right without linkages to the service sector and beyond. Therefore, Local Content Policies (LCPs), strategies and actions force international companies involved in extractive industries to use local companies to supply goods and services. These LCPs, frameworks and actions also force these companies to invest in facilities for local manufacturing and service provision (Ovadia, 2014).

When developed and implemented well, Local Content Frameworks (LCFs) are generally believed to foster development. The benefit that accrue to countries in terms of capital retained in the local economy as a result of local content has the potential to be larger than the royalties and taxes from extraction of a particular resource. The positive outcomes from LCFs require strong state governance and long term investment by both the state and the private sector which sometimes seem to be burdensome to the actors particularly the International Oil Companies (IOCs). Nevertheless, the long-term benefits are desirable which include among others: lower transportation costs, lower costs associated with expatriate staffing, smoother-flowing supplies of goods and services, greater skills and experience for workers and managers, a strengthened relationship with the host government and a strengthened social license to operate (Ovadia, 2014). What is clear from the rationale for local content is that the value-add from it will not happen overnight. However the long-term advantages of enhanced local development, alongside the empowerment of a generation to participate directly in their nation's wealth of resource, are well worth pursuing. The ultimate aim is simple: to ensure that natural resources are not a curse but a blessing, bringing sustainable social and economic benefits within the oil and gas sector and the wider economy (Easo and Wallace, 2014).

However, the implementation of local content policies can produce negative effects when increasing the participation of the local industry such as consuming wealth rather that creating value, attracting high cost investors and inferior industry development. There are also social impacts like demographic change associated with in-migration, concentration of economic activity around the project area, changes in patterns of land use, and institutional change which may compromise the existing sources of livelihoods.

Experiences from Latin America and the Broader African Setting

Experiences and evidence regarding local content policies and practices are mixed and expected outcomes depend on a series of factors such as local content policy design (Nordas et al., 2003). Different outcomes have been achieved by countries depending on the frameworks they adopt to promote local content. Nonetheless, there are other factors that influence the outcomes of local content such as the ability to enforce these frameworks, the economic and social environment of the country, available technology, well-functioning National Oil Companies and monitoring Boards, Enterprise centers, and transparency, among others.

Of these factors recent research (Morales et al., 2016; Mushemeza et al., 2017), identify factors that matter most. Indeed, the importance of well-designed local content frameworks, strong NOCs and a business friendly environment when achieving local content outcomes for oil and gas producing countries in Latin America has been advanced (Morales et al., 2016). After running a model to identify the correlation between the factors that might influence the development of local content, this conclusion has been supported (Kazzazi and Nouri, 2012). Their analysis shows a positive correlation (the highest among the variables of their study) between local content policies and local content development (Kazzazi & Nouri, 2012). It has been argued that well-designed LCFs, the presence of International Financing Institutions (IFIs) such as the World Bank, and the presence of local content monitoring entities – such as enterprise centres and monitoring boards – are important factors that shape local content outcomes in Africa, especially in Angola and Nigeria (Mushemeza and Okiira, 2016a).

There is evidence that oil and gas producing countries have established different types of frameworks to foster local content through the promotion of employment, skills development and national industry participation (Mushemeza and Okiira, 2016a). These frameworks vary from broader national policies articulated in National Development Plans, different types of legislation (local content laws, percentages in terms of procurement and supplies by local firms, decrees, regulations, etc.), and special considerations in contracts to local firms. Experiences from other countries draw lessons on how these frameworks have been implemented in diverse scenarios. Nevertheless, when establishing a local content policy, each country has a different approach depending on its context and necessities. In this sense, local content cannot be applied in the same way in every country due to the diversity of contexts and challenges that they face. This means that there is not a "local content manual" that countries can exactly replicate.

Brazil, Colombia, Trinidad and Tobago, Angola, Ghana, Equatorial Guinea and Nigeria are examples of countries from Latin America and Africa that have established formal local content policies and have implemented these policies for some years. In Brazil local content policies aim at increasing the participation of the national industry on a competitive basis; improve national technological development; improve the level of capabilities and create job opportunities for nationals and achieve growth income (National Petroleum Agency, 2009). LCPs are enabled by an integrated set of tools that include regulations, fiscal incentives, and support programmes.

As a result of adopting specific local content policies, Brazil has successfully increased its local content quotas. In this scenario, Brazil has emerged as an important actor for implementing local content and permanent monitoring of the compliance of local content targets. Bidding processes incorporate local content requirements and designated institutions monitor compliance according to the national local content framework. However, despite the fact that there has been an increase in the creation of jobs and local industries have been strengthened, Brazil has faced challenges due to the costs of implementing its local content policy, production quota delays, a lack of technology and some issues of corruption. Despite this, Brazil has become a reference for other countries in the region when creating and adopting local content frameworks (Mushemeza et al., 2017). In countries such as Bolivia, Colombia and Ecuador there is not a specific legislation for local content in the oil and gas sector. Nonetheless, there are regulations distributed in different frameworks that seek to promote national employment and local sourcing practices. In Ecuador, for instance there are regulations that promote local labor. For example, Article 75 of the Mining Law establishes that the 80 percent of the companies' workforce must be Ecuadorian. Likewise, Article 31 of the Hydrocarbons Law contains a regulation for companies that provide services to EP Petro Ecuador (NOC) that establishes that these companies must hire 90 percent of Ecuadorian citizens for technical positions and 100 percent for the administrative ones (Grupo FARO and ACODE, 2015). In Bolivia the situation is similar to Ecuador. Article 334 of the National Constitution establishes that "the Bolivian state guarantees the preference in the acquisition of materials, for the micro and small enterprises and the productive community organizations". This article has been crucial especially for the gas sector where the State has a strong participation through its National Oil Company (NOC). Furthermore, the Article 15 of the Hydrocarbons Law establishes that 'under no conditions, companies' foreign personnel can exceed the 15 percent of the total share on employees'. In the same way, Article 68 of this law establishes that 'companies that subscribe contracts with NOC must have explicit clauses about preferential process to hire workforce, purchase goods and services and training processes to the NOC's employees' (Petrobras, 2005).

Colombia has no specific regulation or articles in the Hydrocarbons Law. However, the Minerals Law in its Article 253 establishes that the Colombian state invites companies to increase the capacities of the local workers; likewise, Article 254 mentions that the Ministry of Mines and Energy is the authority in charge of designating the percentage of local workers in the extractive activities (Martinez, 2014). Mexico has recently passed a petroleum law that establishes the promotion of 'national content' by Pemex (Mexico's National Oil Company) (Mexican Petroleum Law, 2014). Venezuela has also established articles that promote local content, especially through national industry participation; its Hydrocarbons Law establishes that the Executive must adopt measures that promote the formation of national capital through the incorporation of nationally based companies in the oil sector (Venezuelan Hydrocarbons Law).

In spite of the above shortcomings, the IOCs in Latin America have been able to implement activities that generate jobs and skills development. The examples of Brazil, Trinidad and Tobago, and Mexico drive this point home. In Brazil one major enabler of local content is PROMINP (Programme for the Mobilization of the Oil and Gas Industry) which is financed by the government. The inception of the PROMINP is believed to be the driver behind the boost in the participation of the domestic industry in investments from 57.3 per cent in 2003 to 74.3 per cent in 2010 (Tordo and Anouti, 2013). The National Petroleum Agency (ANP) has been able to publish the value of investment and local content achieved at the item level. There is data on cumulative value of total investment, domestic portion, and percentage local content by item evaluated (Tordo and Anouti, 2013). In Trinidad and Tobago most local content activities have been driven by the private sector. In a Survey carried out to evaluate the satisfaction of T & T's oil and gas service companies with LCPs, results show that 51 per cent of local companies are somewhat satisfied with the government LCPs, and 44 per cent are not satisfied. The establishment of the first specialized fabrication yard in the country in 2004 was seen as a major success story in the implementation of local content (Tordo and Anouti, 2013:172). Similarly, the involvement of experienced IOCs (e.g. British Petroleum) has enabled T & T to register achievements in training nationals in the area of engineering and procurement.

Mexico's local content strategy has focused on the development of its national industries through industrialization programmes. Pemex has developed a comprehensive strategy for the development of providers, contracts and national content including detailed information on the measurement of local content. Pemex has implemented efforts aimed at ensuring that national providers are aware of procurement calls for services. To date, Pemex has been achieving positive outcomes regarding local content, especially in terms of national industry participation. The company has established several programmes with its providers and has a complete register of the contracts awarded to national and local providers. Likewise, Pemex has developed several communication channels to develop capacities among its providers. For example, its website has an entire section devoted to providers in order to include them in bidding process for services and goods (Mushemeza et al., 2017).

The cases of African countries are different in terms of having more focused local content frameworks compared to most Latin American countries. With the support of international financial institutions and International oil companies some, African countries have been able to carry out baseline studies and developed local content policies and legislations. This does not suggest that African countries have performed better in implementation of LCPs and local participation. A brief interrogation of experiences in Tanzania, Angola, Nigeria and Ghana indicate that more is yet to be done to involve citizens, and local companies to realize expected local participation. For instance, in November 2014, Tanzania published a new model Production Sharing Agreement, which tightened local content provisions obliging companies to '*maximize their utilization of goods, services and materials from Tanzania*' and giving priority to nationals. It is up to the industry to create mechanisms and strategies to drive local content development, or in some cases, to circumvent local content requirements. Tanzania is yet to implement these good policies to allow citizens participate fully in the oil and gas sector.

In Angola, local content legislation is clearly identifiable but different laws govern different areas of local content and there is no single institution to supervise enforcement. Various stakeholders, sometimes with conflicting agendas and responsibilities, govern different aspects and compliant status is not achieved at one time. To respond to these challenges, the national Oil Company has been trying to consolidate the lead in the implementation of LCPs particularly, involvement of local companies and skills development through enterprise centers. The main focus of its frameworks is on local employment. These policies have achieved positive outcomes since the number of Angolans involved in the country's oil sector has increased considerably.

Evidence in the literature show that the targets that Angolan authorities set in 1990 were met in 2002 for unskilled workers, exceeded for mid-level staff, and came short by 46 percentage points for higher-skilled staff. Overall, the Angolanization rate was 77 per cent. By 1999 the total number of workers had increased to 10,061 while Angolanization rates remained similar to the 1990 levels. In 2002 the total number of Angolan workers increased by around 35 percentage points from the 1999 levels. Compared with 1990, the overall Angolanization rate increased to 88 per cent (Tordo and Anouti, 2013).

In the case of Nigeria, the Nigerian Content Development and Monitoring Board (NCDMB) estimates that local capture of oil industry spend has gone from 5 per cent to 40 per cent in the last decade. It is estimated that with an annual investment of US$ 15 billion per year, local content would be retaining over US$ 5 billion in the Nigerian economy annually. Manufacturing has increased from 1.9 percent of GDP to 9 percent according to NBS figures of 2014. Nigeria has introduced several measures with the objective of increasing local value added, employment and ownership in the petroleum sector as well as in the industrial sector more generally. However, some scholars believe that the considerable oil revenues flowing into Nigeria over the past four decades have not been translated into adequate infrastructure, social services or an enabling environment for industrial development (Nordas et al., 2003).

Ghana has also recently adopted formal local content policies. The main aim of these policies is to enable locals to participate in 90 percent of exploitation processes. The objectives of local content in oil and gas are defined in the 2009-2010 National Energy Policy and the corresponding regulations set out in the Petroleum Commission Act 2011 (Act 821 and 2013 Regulation) (Amoako et al., 2015). The objectives of the National Energy Policy 2009-2010 include maximizing the benefits of wealth generated through oil and gas, building local capability in all aspects of the oil and gas value chain through education, skills and expertise development, transfer of technology and know-how, increasing international competitiveness of local businesses, creating oil and gas and related industries to sustain economic development and developing an active research and development portfolio. Ghana is yet to measure the outcomes of the implementation of the frameworks. It will also require independent researchers to verify the claims of such measurement. Nevertheless, According to Ghana National Petroleum Company (GNPC), there is high involvement of Ghanaians in offshore and onshore activities providing services but the industry is extremely capital intensive and not easy to mobilise financial resources from financial institutions. Local companies remain limited to ancillary services like real estate and hospitality; they are not yet competitive, lack industry certification, and face high costs of doing business. IOCs still import some foods.

There are also few gains in procurement where over 150 Ghanaian companies are operating in the upstream sector and total contracts awarded amount to $600m since 2009. On employment and training, there is no follow up yet and there are no statistics on how much human power goes directly into oil and gas and what percentage goes to other sectors of the economy. Furthermore, although GNPC established a fund for capacity development through scholarships, there is no evidence of a coordinated approach to capacity development among oil companies (Amoako *et al.*, 2015).

Furthermore, Oil companies were supposed to prepare and implement plans for technology transfer, however, it is too early to tell whether this has been carried out. Skills training have been provided at Takoradi Polytechnic and Kwame Nkrumah University. There has been no follow-up on students trained and where they are going for jobs, what percentage of trained manpower goes to other areas of the economy (Amoako *et al*, 2015).

Lessons from Experiences in Latin America and Selected African Countries

Adoption of local content frameworks - From the analysis done by ACODE (Uganda) and Grupo FARO (Ecuador) under the project Evidence and Lessons from Latin America and Africa, (ELLA),it is evident that countries that have adopted and implemented specific local content frameworks (LCFs) for quite some time i.e. entrenched local content provisions in policies, laws and contracts; have registered better outcomes in terms of skills developed, jobs created and participation of local companies and citizens generally in oil and gas supply chain. Examples include Brazil, Mexico, Columbia, Angola, and Nigeria. In other words, specificity of the LCF matter in the design of local content frameworks.

Joint assessment of existing capacities against the needs of the oil and gas companies –Assessment of a country's existing capacities against the needs of the oil and gas companies is an important and good practice. Studying the match between needs and available resources helps to narrow the potential for immediate local participation and identify the gaps which need to be filled over time with specific programmes.

Establishing a relationship between companies and local business partners – This practice can mediate local participation and identify the gaps which need to be filled over time with specific programmes. In 2011, a system was designed to provide a comprehensive database of Nigerian contractors and competencies. In Angola, contractors need to ensure that the training programme results in transfer of technology and know-how. A fund for the promotion of Entrepreneurship was established in 2008 to support the creation of local companies. Enterprise centres are critical in both Nigeria and Angola for skills development to enable local participation.

Setting realistic targets of local content- Brazil has avoided setting unrealistic local content targets because they believe it could harm them by undermining the competitiveness of the sector. They opt for gradual building up the local content share. This means countries must build the capacity to measure local content. African countries have so far not done well on this point. National aggregate Data on what has been achieved is limited.

Creating an enabling environment for the capacity to measure local content – Experiences from Colombia where there is enabling environment to monitor and evaluate local content impacts, have better outcomes from implementation of LCPs (Morales *et al*, 2016).

African and Latin American experiences show that common local content strategies are employment, skills development and national Industry participation. The tendency in most Africa experiences show that beyond employment, skills development and national industry participation, tax incentives that have employment seem to push these countries to opt for short term strategies to address unemployment crisis. In Brazil, Mexico and Columbia the priority is in national industry participation. These countries prioritise skilling the citizens and improving the competences of local companies to become competitive on the market. This means a country that prioritises local participation of its citizens is likely to achieve more in terms of skills developed and eventually more jobs created.

It is clear from the above narrative that in Africa where LCF have been fully developed the implementation is still wanting. There is need to emphasize national industry participation by creating an enabling environment and incentives to local companies, establishing institutions for skills development and technology transfer if jobs are to be created to address the unemployment crisis. It also clear from the literature that there are no national statistics that show the LCF outcomes. The information available is scattered and not update. For those countries still developing their frameworks, there is much more to learn particularly, having a clear LC policy and legislation, making detailed contracts with specific LC requirements, and make governance of the sector transparent and accountable.

Limitations to Local Participation in Uganda

Local participation is expressed in terms of involvement of the key stakeholders in the economy. The successful formulation and implementation of local content framework depends on how various stakeholders work together. Indeed various stakeholders contribute different perspectives, skills and resources that aid successful formulation and implementtation. In the case of Uganda, the key stakeholders are the government, private sector, CSOs, IOCs and the communities where the resource is extracted. It is therefore important to identify the major hindrances to local participation particularly in relation to the private sector, CSOs and the communities.

We have already indicated that LCFs include policies, legislations, contracts and actions a country undertake to enhance the capacity of its citizens to take advantage of the opportunities in the oil and gas industry. The questions that arise now are what are the bottlenecks that hinder effective participation? What interventions are necessary to mitigate those hindrances?

First, the majority of citizens and the key local stakeholders do not have sufficient information on the investment opportunities in the oil and gas sector. This is complicated by the mindset that the oil industry is complicated and requires a lot of capital. Yet producing items such as food that will feed the workers in the forthcoming development stage does not require a lot of funds. In any case over the decades Ugandans have been supplying food stuffs to neighboring countries such as South Sudan and Eastern Democratic Republic of Congo and Rwanda.

Second, the studies that have been made and the findings in form of needs assessment, capabilities, industry opportunities etc. are still not adequately disseminated in a language and form that can reach the majority of population. These reports need to be transformed into short and simple materials and newspaper articles in various languages for citizens to access information.

In the light of the above bottlenecks the following strategic policy actions are critical to enhance local participation.

Participatory approach to development of local content policies, strategies and programmes: Stakeholder participation is always critical in developing policies and programmes for their benefit. When citizens are involved in such process, they own the outcome and eventually develop a consciousness to implement the agendas. Uganda has a network of active CSOs, organized communities in the Albertine region and associations that represent the private sector such as (Uganda Chamber of Commerce and Industry, Private Sector Foundation, Uganda manufacturers Association) which should be involved as the country improves its local content framework.

At the minimum, the policy and strategies should have core principles that focus on: work force development; employment of local work force; and training of local work force; investments in supplier development; developing supplies and services locally; and procuring supplies and services locally. The proposed policy for Uganda emphasizes capacity building, procurement of locally produced or available goods and services; employment of Ugandan citizens; technology transfer, research and development; measurement and monitoring of national content.

Local content policies ought to be supported by legislations that operationalises local content principles. This among other things includes creation of required institutional structures and allocation of roles. The contracts between IOCs and the government or sub-contractors should be clear on the responsibilities of each party on implementation of local content rather than depending on the good will of the IOCs through the corporate social responsibility (CSR) principle as has been the case in some countries.

Once the LCP is in place, the implementation should be guided by five key strategies as articulated (Mireftekhari, 2013). These strategies are critical in addressing three key broad variables- skills development, industrial participation and employment.

Joint venture with local firms: Local firms can gain substantial capacity development benefits through working as a partner or subcontractor with international firms. Similarly it can increase opportunities for knowledge and technology transfer.

Training and skills development of local work force: Both the general education and specialist skills are applicable but should be based on a detailed analysis of local capabilities and a schedule of the skill requirements over the life of the resource. It is therefore, important to have a strategy that consist programmes about basic education, locally-appropriate methods, and practical experience, flexibility, and scholarship schemes.

Developing local education and training institutions: Enhancing a local institute has more effect than it seems. It has added advantages of supporting wider skills development in the local economy and promoting the companies' long-term reputation as a good corporate citizen.

Industry collaboration: Industry collaboration can cause enterprise development. For instance, the CAE – a Business Support Centre is part of the Angolan Ministry of petroleum which has the objective to promote the participation and sustainable development of Small and medium Enterprises (SMEs) in the Angolan Oil industry. Similar enterprises have been established in Nigeria, Chad, Ghana and Equatorial Guinea with positive and impressive outcomes. The plan to establish a national industry enhancement center the equivalent of enterprise centres in Angola, Nigeria and Chad is positive and would promote national participation.

Local procurements: The strategy should aim at improving local procurement by providing additional information, reducing the size and complexity of the scope, or simplifying procedures or processes to make it more likely that local firms will participate in the procurement process.

The Industrial Baseline Survey (IBS) in Uganda identified twenty five sectors with high potential for local content (transportation, and logistics, food supply, domestic waste management, facility management, manpower agency, work safety products, road construction, among others). These are sectors which are less technical and where local capacity exists. Yet only two sectors (security and cement manufacturing) among the twenty five meet the oil and gas standards and have a quantity gap of 10 per cent. It is therefore important for Uganda to make regulations and contracts that have provisions that enable support of those sectors through e.g. matching grants for technology improvement, quality certification, infrastructure interventions benefiting these sectors, and dedicated financing programmes (World Bank Group, 2015).

The government of Uganda can also take actions in the financial sector to promote local participation such as the creation of incentives. The government should consider providing incentives in terms of soft loans to the upcoming enterprises to enable them participate in the oil industry. This is possible through numerous Cooperative Savings and credit societies that exist throughout the country. This would however require addressing the issue of interest rates, which still remain high in the traditional commercial Banks and savings and credit associations.

It is important to note that Local companies have host of challenges ranging from access to affordable credit to the requisite skills to turn around their business fortunes. Consequently fiscal incentives will be necessary to enable local companies to develop capacity. Tax incentives must be considered for companies establishing facilities to manufacture goods or provide services that would otherwise be imported. The tendency in Uganda has been to have a soft spot for foreigners in terms of investment opportunities and this undermines local participation. A criterion therefore must be put in place to determine deserving companies in order to avoid abusing the power to grant such incentives.

Accessing affordable credit is indeed one of the challenges that face local suppliers. The government should therefore identify and implement reforms to strengthen financial infrastructure that support local investments in the oil and gas sector. For instance it is possible to set up credit lines and risk sharing facilities for oil and gas suppliers; and also availing training to suppliers to prepare financial statements and loan applications. The proposed Industry Enhancement Centre would be appropriate to take such a function. Similarly development partners would be invited to support such initiatives. While making the implementation of LCPs possible the World Bank Group partnering with the governments of Angola, Chad and Nigeria; civil society organizations, and the UNDP put up enterprise centres that are making the implementation of LCPs and local participation a reality (Mushemeza and Okiira, 2016b).

The Uganda government should prepare for the coexistence between oil and tourism. Oil development that compromises other livelihood opportunities is undesirable. Tourism being one of the long-term drivers of Uganda's economy, any disruption to it should be avoided. When oil revenues are utilized to strengthen the tourist attractions rather destroying them, the citizens will reap the benefits of diversification. It is established that 40 per cent of Uganda's known oil reserves are found in the Murchison Falls National Park (MFNP), one of the most popular parks in the country, certainly there will be a lot of congestion in the park and surrounding areas coming from the oil workers and movement of machinery, causing disturbance for animals and tourists. It is important for the government of Uganda and its relevant agencies, Departments lower local governments (Ministry of Tourism and Wild Life, Uganda's Wild life Authority, Uganda Tourism Board, local governments) to ensure appropriate measures are taken to minimize disruption at MFNP while activities are ongoing and affected sites are restored following the completion of activities. For instance, it is possible to engage cross-sector stakeholders and foster collaboration; enhance existing tourism offerings; conduct periodic surveys of tourists' experience in the park; issue legislations and regulations; and provide infrastructure in the park necessary for separation of oil activities from tourism.

Uganda should integrate cross cutting issues in the local content framework particularly human rights and HIV/AIDS. This requires designing appropriate programmes for sensitization of the communities and actors engaged in the activities associated with exploration, extraction and transportation of the oil and the related products. Local participation would be meaningless if the population is sick, and the rights of citizens are not respected by powerful actors in the sub-sector. Workers' rights should be respected and protected as the oil and gas industry expands.

Furthermore, there is need for a robust monitoring framework for the local content policy implementation. Having Local Content Policy and relevant legislation is good, but true value –add is impossible without effective monitoring and enforcement mechanisms. There is need therefore for a robust institutional and monitoring framework to implement the local content requirements and programmes. In order to address Local Content and Local participation monitoring requirements, Nigeria established Nigeria Content Development and Monitoring Board (NCDMB), while Ghana and Tanzania have put in place Local Content Monitoring Committees (LCMCs) with mandate to monitor and coordinate all aspects of implementing local content policy and legislation. It should be noted however, that the effectiveness of the monitoring committees or Board whatever the case may be, will largely dependent on its independence in operations and accountability mechanisms.

Local participation should not end in policy documents. Rather a robust monitoring framework with clear targets and timelines need to be developed to continuously assess steps and actions being taken. The more local companies and citizens participate in the oil and gas supply chain especially during the forthcoming development stage (construction of the refinery, pipeline etc.), the more likely they would feel that oil and gas are for them and that the country will have escaped from the popular perception of resource curse in Africa.

Conclusion

We have argued that oil and gas producing countries particularly in Africa and Latin America have over the years adopted local content frameworks (policies, laws and contracts designed to generate further benefits from extractive industries beyond the direct contribution of its value-added)) in order to exploit their natural resource. Local content strategy is preferred because it is expected to increase local participation through increased skills and technology transfer, involvement of local companies and citizens and generation of jobs.

Experiences in both Africa and Latin America have been drawn for Uganda to learn from. It has been established that countries that adopt local content frameworks with clear and entrenched provisions on local content (specificity) in policies, laws and contracts are more likely to register better outcomes in terms of skills developed, participation of local companies and generation of jobs for citizens. This must however go hand in hand with well-functioning and implementation institutions such as national oil companies, Enterprise Centres, monitoring and measuring Boards as factors that matter most. There are also other factors that cannot be ignored such as an enabling business environment, sector governance, (transparency and accountability and zero tolerance to corruption).

It was also argued that although Uganda has a progressive draft local content policy as a starting point, care must be taken to increase awareness and ultimately ownership of policy once it has been adopted and published. This is because the initiation and formulation did not engage as much stakeholders as it should have been. Similarly, the policy is not enough to guarantee effective participation. This must be followed by an enabling legislation and detailed contracts that commit companies involved in the sector to implement local content provisions that enhance local participation, economic diversification and a better quality of life of the people the ultimate objective of local content strategy in natural resources endowed countries.

References

Amoako, T., Aubynn, T. and Atta- Quayson, A. (2015) *Local Content Policies in the Oil and Gas Sectors: Is Ghana Getting it Right?* Accra: ACET.

Easo, J. and Wallace, A. (2014) *Understanding Local Content Policies in Africa's Petroleum Sector.* Texas: Andrews Kurth.

Esteves, A. N., Coyne, B. and Moreno, A. (2013) 'Enhancing the Subtancial Benefits of the Oil, Gas and Mining Sectors, Natural Resource Governance Institute'. New York.

Grupo FARO and ACODE (2015) 'Design and Methods Paper: Local Content Frameworks in Latin American and African Oil and Gas Sector'. Evidence and Lessons from Latin America (ELLA). Available at: http://www.eisourcebook.org/cms/December.

Heum, P., Kasande, R., Ekern, O. and Nyombi, A. (2011) *Policy and Regulatory Frameworks to Enhance Local Content. Institute for Research in Economics and Business Administration.* Bergen.

Kazzazi, A. and Nouri, B. (2012) 'A Conceptual Model for Local Content Development in the Petroleum Industry', *Management Science Letters*, pp. 2165–2174.

Martínez, M. (2014) 'Impacto Economico Local de las Industrias Extractivas en Colombia'. Bogota.

Mireftekhari, S. P. (2013) *Local Content Strategy, Solution for Successful Global Oil and Gas projects in Emerging Economies.* , Norwegian University of Science and Technology.

Morales, M., Herrera, J. and Jarrin, S. (2016) *Local Content Frameworks in Latin American Oil and Gas Sectors: Lessons from Ecuador and Colombia.* ELLA Programme. Practical Action Latin America, Lima and Grupo Faro, Quito.

Mushemeza, E. D. and Okiira, J. (2016a) 'Getting More out of the Oil and Gas Sector: Lessons from Angola and Chad', *ACODE Policy Briefing Paper.* Kampala, 35.

Mushemeza, E. D. and Okiira, J. (2016b) *Local Content Frameworks in African Oil and Gas Sector: Lessons from Angola and Chad.* ELLA Programme. Practical Action Latin America, Lima and ACODE.

Mushemeza, Okiira, Morales and Herrera (2017) 'What Matters When it Comes to Adopting Local Content? A Comparative Analysis of Success Factors in Africa and Latin America', *ACODE Policy Research Series.* Kampala, 79.

National Petroleum Agency (2009) *Local Content: Goals and Brief History.* Rio de Janeiro: ANP.

Nordas, H., Vatne, E. and Heum, P. (2003) *The Upstream Petroleum Industry and Local Industrial Development: A Comparative Study.* Bergen:

Institute for Research in Economics and Business Administration.

Ovadia, J. (2014) 'Local Content and Natural Resource Governance: The Cases of Angola and Nigeria', *The Extractive Industries and Society*, pp. 137–146.

Petrobras (2005) 'Bolivian Hydrocarbons Law', No. 3058. Available at: http://www.wikinvest.com/stock/Petrobras_(PBR)/New_Hydrocarbons_Law_Bolivia.

Tordo, S. and Anouti, Y. (2013) *Local Content in the Oil and Gas Sector: Case Studies*. Washington DC: World Bank.

World Bank Group (2015) 'Leveraging Oil and Gas Industry for the Development of a Comparative Private Sector in Uganda'. Washington D. C: World Ban

CHAPTER FOUR

Resolving Petroleum Conflicts in Uganda's Albertine Graben

Sebastiano Rwengabo

Introduction

Africa is susceptible to the unfortunate association between the oil and gas industry and conflicts (Watts, 2001). How, then, can nascent petroleum economies prevent and/or manage oil-driven conflicts within the petro-state, and, in some contexts, between states? Addressing this question requires as assessment of conflict resolution mechanisms in a given polity. Intra-state conflicts can erupt within and between communities, between local governance authorities, between preexisting traditional authority structures and the central slate, and between local and central governments. The level, intensity, and trajectory of conflicts depend upon each country's specific sociopolitical configurations, such as governance infrastructure and nature of intra-society and state-society relations. Interstate, cross-border, conflicts can erupt when oil and gas deposits are found along shared international boundaries, and/or when oil-related developments have direct bearing on a neighboring country. Conflicts arise because, petroleum wealth, like other high-value natural-resources, tends to distort the country's economy, through resource dependence, leading to economic collapse and unemployment that engender civil strife. Certain characteristics of high-value resources, determine these resources' conflict linkages: relative location, socioeconomic linkages, lootability of resources (Ross, 2003) like gold vis-a-vis petroleum, the role and interest of external actors (consider Chad during the 1970s) (Humphreys, 2005), ruling elites' tendency to violently counter threats to their control over lucrative opportunities (Swanson, 2002), and feasibility of armed conflict vis-a-vis non-armed opposition (Collier *et al.*, 2009). Given these multiple factors, consensus remains elusive on managing oil conflicts. It remains unclear when and how conflict-management practices like conflict early warning, prevention, detection, resolution, and transformation can be adopted to ensure enduring peace within and between petroleum-endowed economies.

Existing studies are inconclusive on the mechanisms through which petroleum conflicts can be managed. The governance argument presupposes that improving the country's governance prevents conflicts since oil and gas wealth tends to engender non-transparent governance and fuel elite corruption, oil looting, and violence against the opposition (Swanson, 2002). Thus, government self-restraint can prevent violence escalation. This view seems to absolve oil companies' role in causing and resolving conflicts. It does not address conflict prevention measures but stresses reactive–as opposed to preventative–conflicts management. The thesis also ignores the cross-border dimension of oil-and-gas-driven conflicts. The resource dependence thesis avers that reversing overdependence on petroleum wealth can allow a country to reduce resource-driven conflicts. According to Collier, when comparing countries that depends on primary commodity exports, risks of conflict are greater as the percent of GDP reliance on that commodity increases. For example, conflict potential rises to 33 per cent when the natural-resource exports are at least 25 per cent of GDP (Collier, 2003). Other studies argue that natural resource dependence prolongs pre-existing conflicts (Fearon and Laitin, 2003).Hence, minimizing this dependence reduces conflict potentialities: this demands conflict prevention and/or resolution through productive diversification. The final proposition, the *weak state thesis,* indicates that grievance over past natural resource mismanagement leads to future conflicts, displaying strong association with civil wars (Ross, 2003). Humphreys claims that natural resource wars tend to end with military victory of one side over another– underlining the military approach to conflict resolution. But divergent, sometimes conflicting, interests from foreign and domestic actors may lead to protracted conflicts.

First, petroleum conflicts can be endemic whether or not they have escalated to violence and depending on the actors involved as Nigeria's experience demonstrate. Second, transnational oil cartels can elude weak states' controls, being financially stronger than weak states, connected to ruling elites in developed societies, and are able to finance private military-security infrastructure to protect their interests. Where these cartels are parties to conflicts, resolution may necessitate engagement of external state parties. In fact some of these multinational cartels may be linked with the "a new scramble for African oil" (Frynas and Paulo, 2007), constituting the nexus between oil and national security interests of foreign states (Klare and Volman, 2006). Third, the potential for foreign-linked "petro-violence" (Watts, 2001) and "the dirty politics of African oil" (Shaxson, 2007) is rendered complex when bloody conflicts over oil and gas exploitation (Ross, 2008) exceed the conflict-prevention and de-escalation stage. Consequently, conflicts have been receding but have persisted in oil-rich countries because "oil wealth often wreaks havoc on a country's economy and politics, makes it easier for insurgents to fund their rebellions, and aggravates ethnic grievances" (Ross, 2008). Finally, understanding conflict management in nascent oil and gas economies requires an analysis of preexisting conflicts through a situational analysis of the complex interplay of different factors within in a polity.

This chapter analyses petroleum-driven conflicts within and between neighboring states, herein "intrastate" and "cross-border" conflicts. It draws on the findings of qualitative field and desk research on Uganda's nascent oil and gas sector, and examines petroleum-driven conflicts within Uganda, though appreciation is made of conflicts between Uganda and Democratic Republic of Congo (DRC), especially misgivings in the DRC about developments in Uganda's oil and gas sector. Inherent in the analysis are proposals for policy-relevant measures for preventing and, where they arise, resolving petroleum conflicts. The chapter argues that while Uganda is conflict-prone, the petroleum sector has exacerbated existing conflicts in the Albertine Graben and may generate new ones within the country and between the two neighboring states whose relations have previously been un-cordial. The development and operationalization of multilevel conflict-resolution mechanisms is vital for detecting, mitigating, de-escalating, and resolving future conflicts. In terms of policy and practice, intra-state conflicts will require intra-state conflict-resolution mechanisms. Cross-border conflicts can be resolved through bilateral and regional mechanisms. The rest of the chapter addresses the link between oil and gas wealth and intra-state and inter-state/cross-border conflicts, before analyzing extant conflicts in Uganda's Albertine Graben and the mechanisms for resolving them before concluding.

The Link between Oil and Conflicts

Channels of oil-driven conflicts are not hard to demonstrate. Richard Auty outlined a "two-stage process" through which natural resources generate civil strife, leading to cumulative research linking natural resource endowment and civil conflict. One view states that natural resources *create incentives for war entrepreneurship*, hence rebel greed, not objective grievance, leads to civil war (Collier *et al.*, 2009). Quantitative correlations between natural resource endowments and armed conflicts were revealed, though deeper analyses found factors like state capacity, role and interest of external actors (Humphreys, 2005), lootability of natural resources (Ross, 2003), ruling elites' tendency to violently crush threats to their control of lucrative wealth (Swanson, 2002), and feasibility of armed conflict vis-a-vis non-armed opposition, to be important (Collier *et al.*, 2009). The resulting knowledge about natural resource conflicts has attracted policy attention.

Oil conflicts may result from *over-dependence on oil wealth*. According to Collier, the higher the natural-resource dependence the higher is the likelihood of conflict. Dependence on primary commodity exports ranging around 5 per cent of GDP generates a 6 per cent risk of conflict. When, however, natural-resource exports are 25 per cent of GDP the chance of conflict rises to 33 per cent (Collier, 2003). The problem is less about availability; it is about dependence, on natural resources. But since humanity depends on natural resources, and has historically developed technologies for making efficient exploitation of nature, the difference between *resource availability* and *resource dependence* is only analytic: even those societies which are less endowed with lucrative natural resources, such as oil, minerals, fertile soils, depend on those same resources which they exploit from distant lands. The whole habitable world, then, falls under the same bracket when considering the man-nature relationship.

The issue is not necessarily about where resources are located or not, but *whether they are contentious*. Contentions about access to oil is one other mechanism for oil conflict. Resource conflicts afflicting natural-resource-endowed geo-social spaces are in no way unconnected with distant societies lacking such endowments; those distant societies may be–and always are–involved in these conflicts due to desire to access these resources. It follows, therefore, that whether or not those conflicts appear to be intra-societal (intra-state), they are intricately connected to the broad international political economy of natural resource access and exploitation. Other studies argue that where [resource] conflicts already exist, resource dependence prolongs them (Fearon and Laitin, 2003).

The *weak state mechanism* focuses on conflict onset. It avers that conflict onset responds more to past natural resource production than to future production, stressing grievance over past mismanagement of natural resources (Humphreys, 2005). While resonating with the view that natural resources, diamonds and drugs are correlated with civil wars (Ross, 2003), the mechanism highlights grievance over natural resource mismanagement contrary to the greed-grievance thesis which undervalues objective grievance. Humphreys claims that foreigners have interest in working to bring natural resource-related armed conflicts to an end when their natural resource supplies are under threat. This assumes convergence of foreigners' interests and/or non-complicity in such conflicts. Considering divergent, sometimes conflicting interests from foreign and domestic actors, we hardly trust this argument. Humphreys also ignores two theoretical and empirical realities of today's world.

First, *liberalization and marketization of military services* and production makes resource conflicts endemic as companies' operations in weak states tend to fuel conflicts (Alao, 2007) and create "blood barrels" (Ross, 2008). Second, oil cartels are transnational. They are financially stronger than many weak states. Many of them are politically connected to ruling elites in developed societies. Interested more in profit maximization than socio-economic transformation of the societies in which they operate, these cartels elude weak states' controls, financing their own private military-security infrastructure to protect their interests and creating unique scramble for oil (Frynas and Paulo, 2007) in which foreign national security interests may be discernible (Klare and Volman, 2006). The resulting "dirty politics" of oil (Shaxson, 2007) or "blood barrels" (Ross, 2003) is hardly a domestic or cross-border political economy affair. As petro-exploitation generates grievances in affected societies over environmental destruction and marginalization, conflicts break out at different levels as multinationals are perceived to collude with local elites to deprive affected communities. Thus, "oil wealth often wreaks havoc on a country's economy and politics, makes it easier for insurgents to fund their rebellions, and aggravates ethnic grievances" (Ross, 2008). From the Albertine Graben indicates this challenge.

Conflicts in Uganda's Albertine Graben

Oil-driven conflicts are tensions that followed the announcement of commercial oil and gas reserves in the Albertine Rift with petroleum as a defining element in their expression and metamorphosis. Intra-state conflicts range from political disagreements to land-related and environmental tensions. They include tensions over revenue sharing, and over oil-related decision-making, land acquisitions, resettlements and compensations. The border tensions between Uganda and DRC are beyond my scope. Since major oil and gas exploration activities began, government has expressed commitment to utilize petroleum revenues to equitably benefit Ugandans. But Uganda suffers governance challenges that negate this promise, reducing it to rhetoric unless future developments prove otherwise. Besides technical soundness of a nation's policy and fiscal regimes, judicious management of petro-wealth is a function of the quality of governance. Oil and conflicts in the region erupted even before the country started production.

Oil conflicts would not be unique to Uganda, making this analysis relevant to other cases. Disagreements between South Sudan and Sudan over oil sharing agreements, and experiences from countries like Nigeria, Chad, Cameroun, and Angola, indicate similar trends. Uganda's experience of civil wars, coups, and political instability is a central defining element of public debates about oil and gas politics. Her politico-military edifice, key to oil-related decision-making, projects its influence through civilian institutions and foreign policy, thereby potentially militarizing oil and gas developments. Besides, unresolved tensions with DRC, following which futile attempts were made to undertake joint exploration and resource sharing between the two countries, indicate little progress toward a conflict-free petroleum sector.

Cases of Community-Level Conflicts

Community-level conflicts erupted following the announcement of commercial reserves. They revolve around: land; impact on community livelihood; communities' benefits from, and participation in oil-related activities; the environmental impact of oil exploitation; and historical injustices. Evidence from the Graben indicates "ad hoc and fragmented modes of resource governance" (van Alstine *et al.*, 2014), particularly regarding transparency in these processes. Conflicts first broke out when large-scale land acquisition, mainly for the construction of the refinery in Kabaale Parish, Buseruka sub-county, Hoima district, led to massive evictions without sufficient compensation and sensitization about alternative livelihoods. Subsequently, new conflicts also erupted: Bunyoro leaders were "angered by longstanding land disputes and the government's continued refusal to reveal plans for oil revenue sharing" (Wikileaks, 2009), fusing pre-existing conflicts with petroleum prospects.

Bunyoro-Kitara Kingdom, in whose territorial jurisdiction a large part of the Graben is located, has disagreed with government over the 1 per cent royalties and other benefits from petro-extraction in the kingdom. Whereas existing laws regulate the functioning of Cultural Institutions, stipulate their mandate and relationship with government (Republic of Uganda, 2011a), this conflict indicated a level of conflict transcending tensions at community level. The kingdom's other demands include: land and natural resources (including petroleum), participation in decision making regarding oil and gas investments, petro-revenue management, payment of royalties, and employment of the Kingdom's people. The kingdom also opposed the undervaluing of people's crops during petroleum-driven land compensations. A kingdom minister was temporarily detained in December 2014, after violent eruptions in Rwengabi village, Hoima district, in which 70 houses were burnt, many animals slaughtered, several acres of crops slashed and others uprooted. This wave of violence that saw several local leaders arrested (Mugerwa, 2014) followed violent evictions in Rwamutonga in August 2014.

While Article 244(2) of the constitution states that "Minerals, mineral ores and petroleum shall be exploited taking into account the interests of the individual land owners, local governments and the Government", it was observed that "Tullow Oil dealt directly with the central government for its land, reportedly displacing villagers and creating anxieties among those who feared they would be next. 'Communities living in the oil rich areas complained that they are threatened with eviction when compensation arrangements are not clear" (International Crisis Group, 2012a). As early as 2011, local demands evolved into protests, when "residents of Buliisa blocked the road between an oil well and Tullow Oil's camp, and in 2012 the roads leading to Kibaale were blocked" (Moore, 2013). A local youth group, Bunyoro Local Oil Advocacy Group (BLOAG), advocating oil benefits for local communities, and was put under surveillance over inciting protests (Mugerwa and Muzoora, 2014), adding itself to tensions between the kingdom and government.

The initial non-involvement of the kingdom in oil-related activities, and the claim that the kingdom was initially not considered for payment of royalties (Moore, 2013) led to open conflict. This was inconsistent with Uganda's oil policy, which "recognizes the role to be played by local governments, civil society organisations and cultural institutions through advocacy, mobilisation and dialogue with communities" (Republic of Uganda, 2013). A study of ethno-political mobilisation in Bunyoro over oil and gas wealth reveals that "respondents born in Hoima District were more likely to believe that Bunyoro Kingdom should receive a share of oil revenues, as were those born in Bunyoro districts other than Hoima" (Moore, 2013). Although Moore derogatively presents Banyoro leaders as "tribal leaders"—a view that is inconsistent with the level of development and sociopolitical sophistication that pre-colonial Bunyoro-Kitara had acquired, which placed Bunyoro well above any description as a "tribal polity" before British colonial invasion—her findings indicate fusion between politics, ethnicity, and region in Uganda's evolving oil and gas conflicts despite reserves outside of Bunyoro-Kitara kingdom. This ethno-politicization may generate new tensions (Kathman and Shannon, 2011).

Uganda Human Rights Commission (UHRC) uncovered several tensions in the region. People's concerns "were mainly regarding compensation for land that government was acquiring for oil exploration and production activities", while several rights had been violated, including: "the right to property; the right to information; rights of vulnerable people like women, widows, the elderly and children; land rights, the right to a clean and healthy environment; labour rights; freedom of movement; the right to participation; the right to self-determination; the right to food; the right to education; the right to water; and freedom of expression". The Commission concluded that: (a) civic awareness was inadequate, vindicating World Bank's suggestion that "Providing *reliable and timely* information will help significantly in shaping public expectations" and avoiding false expectations and accusations, and managing people's expectations downwards while also improving *transparency and accountability*(World Bank, 2008). (b) Mutual suspicions among different stakeholders were acute. (c) Government and oil companies had not shared responsibilities with local governments and the kingdom, contrary to Section 7(2) of the oil policy. (d) People were not adequately sensitised about their rights in the context of oil developments, indicating absence of human-rights-related capacity building. Districts joined the fray.

District-Related & Intergovernmental Conflicts

Inter-district consensus among oil districts and between them and non-oil districts remains elusive. The Finance Act of 2012 gazetted some "oil districts" (Republic of Uganda, 2012) situated in Bunyoro-Kitara kingdom: Hoima, Buliisa, Masindi, Kibaale, though others are outside (World Bank, 2008) Conflicts involving these oil districts arose over revenue sharing and other benefits, in form of royalties, of petroleum exploration and/or extraction. "Royalties are payments levied on resource exploitation, and are based on either quantity or value of the resource extracted. Under the terms of the PSA's [Production Sharing Agreements] and as contained in the ITA [Income Tax Act], oil companies will pay a royalty on gross oil production, at a rate that varies with the rate of production (the rate ranges between 7 per cent and 12.5 per cent). This policy leaves unanswered one question: catering for non-oil districts. Tensions over allocations of royalties, constitute the broad intra-state "politics of oil", for it is unclear whether royalties will be equitably shared and/or which formula will be used. These conflicts also indicate lack of inter-district consensus on distribution of oil and gas benefits.

Government proposes that: "In order to promote social cohesion and stable investment and production environment, 7 per cent of all royalty revenues shall be set aside for sharing between local governments located in the oil and gas producing areas. The mechanism of sharing these revenues amongst the local governments will take into account intra☐regional fairness, level of production, and sustainability principles."Non-oil districts felt discriminated against, and opposed this plan. The royalties regime became controversial because districts receive funding from central government not according to their natural-resource endowments. Proscovia Salaamu Musumba, the Kamuli district chairperson, told a consultative meeting on oil and gas developments: "The government seeks to look at the country in aggregates and it is using oil to reconfigure the state by creating super states " (Kigambo, 2013) Preferential treatment, she maintains, would fracture the country and endanger national unity. Creating different levies, financing sources and benefits for different districts under one unitary constitution is unconstitutional. Differential funding, non-oil districts argue, is inconsistent with national unity and holistic development. It gainsays the National Oil and Gas Policy (NOGP)'s objective of ensuring *"mutually* beneficial relationships between all stakeholders in the development of a desirable oil and gas sub sector for the country." (Ministry of Energy and Mineral Development, 2017).

These contradictions remain unresolved. The NOGP offers a compensatory arrangement to ensure that "each local government within the region is compensated" for the social costs incurred from petroleum exploitation, "irrespective of the stage of oil activities undertaken in the locality" (Ministry of Energy and Mineral Development, 2017). It remains unclear, however, how such costs shall be determined, how trans-district costs will be managed and benefits shared, and how non-oil districts shall be compensated for holistic development. World Bank challenges Uganda to "ensure that oil and gas resources (and revenues) are used on the basis of broad national consensus, according to international best practice, and in a transparent and accountable manner for the benefit of all Ugandans": first, by separating petro-revenues from other Government revenues; second, avoiding the use of petroleum revenues for current expenditures; and third, by ensuring that when revenues are used for capital projects, the expenditure is "justified in parliament in accordance with the National Development Plan ." (World Bank, 2009).

Uganda established a *Petroleum Fund* and the *Petroleum Revenue Investment Reserve* managed by Bank of Uganda (Republic of Uganda, 2015b). The law centralises both the Fund and the Reserve. The *Oil and Gas Revenue Management Policy* grants the ministry mandate over the industry, leaving technocrats in the Central Bank and Petroleum Authority to play only supplemental roles .(Ministry of Energy and Mineral Development, 2017). No independent body oversees ministries' activities or regulates their relations with districts (Moore, 2013). Pre-production payments by oil companies have not been adequately communicated to different stakeholders especially districts and the kingdom (Atuhairwe, 2012). Questions over these non-disclosures remain unanswered as are national level tensions.

National Level Conflicts

National level conflicts arise over revenue sharing and policy, and between government and oil companies. The most outstanding *conflict* arose between government and oil companies *over taxation*. In December 2010, a tax dispute broke out between Uganda Revenue Authority (URA) and Heritage Oil and Gas Ltd. Heritage announced its intention to transfer US$ 1.5 million worth of its petroleum assets in Uganda to an Italian company, ENI. However, Tullow Oil had 50 per cent stakes in the assets. It exercised its first right of option under the partnership terms. The URA demanded 30 per cent of the US$1.5 million as capital tax gains tax before approving the transaction. Heritage reportedly followed advice from "leading tax experts in Uganda, United Kingdom and North America" to refuse paying the capital gains tax, forcing the URA to seek legal redress from Uganda's Tax Appeals Tribunal (TAT). Heritage sought to settle the matter in the London-based International Court of Arbitration, while Uganda insisted that the case be settled by the TAT (Republic of Uganda, 2011b). The TAT, in November 2011, upheld URA's assessment of US$ 434.9 million on the capital gains earned by Heritage in the transfer of its interests to Tullow. The Tribunal ordered, among other things, that "The applicants pay capital gains tax of US$ 407,095,366 basing on the evidence adduced before the Tribunal being the amount after the pre-investment relief. The total amount of capital gains tax before the pre-investment relief was US$ 542,793,821", and that "the applicants pay two-thirds (2/3) of the costs of this application to the respondent" (Republic of Uganda, 2011b).

Heritage appealed the TAT's decision in the High Court. It argued, among other issues, that the Tribunal erred in law in holding that its mandate cannot be fettered by a contractual provision in an agreement, praying the High Court to reverse the Tribunal's decision. But Justice Hellen Obura of the High Court held the Tribunal's mandate and decision in the case: "I cannot fault the Tribunal for its findings in which case ground 3 of this appeal also fails ... all the 3 grounds of this appeal fail ... and so the appeal must fail. I accordingly dismiss it with costs and confirmed the decision of the Tribunal" (Republic of Uganda, 2011b). Heritage appealed to the London-based United Nations Commission on International Trade Law (UNCITRAL). The UNCITRAL, in February 2015, ruled in favour of URA, issued a unanimous award dismissing all claims, and ordered Heritage Oil to pay more than $4 million worth of costs incurred by Uganda in connection with the case (Ladu, 2015). These decisions are not inconsistent with the UN resolutions on transparency in treaty-based investor-state arbitration (United Nations, 2014).

The above mentioned case indicates the metamorphosis of oil conflicts and disputes from local to national and international dispute resolution. Though the struggle may seem to have been exclusively judicial, it involved multiple actors at different levels. The changing agency, processes, and outcomes, concurrent with competing interests among these changing actors indicates the complexity and internationality of seemingly national oil-related conflicts. This is where national and international law and agency become close bedfellows in conflict resolution. At the national level, the Finance Bill 2012 disregarded royalties to local beneficiaries. This triggered conflicts that forced government to rectify the question of royalties in the 2015 Public Finance Management Act: "Government shall retain ninety four percent [94 per cent] of the revenue from royalties arising from petroleum production and the remaining six percent [6 per cent] shall be shared among the local governments located within the petroleum exploration and production areas of Uganda" (Republic of Uganda, 2015c).

A newer element of oil conflicts pertains to competition between political coalitions. Petroleum prospects already influenced electoral politics: President Yoweri Museveni proposed ring-fencing some elective positions in oil-rich Bunyoro region for political expediency. The resulting perceived exclusion from petroleum benefits, coupled with failed political institutions threatens to spiral out of control for three reasons: first, as oil and gas wealth is entrenching elite selfish interests without engendering governance efficiency; second, petro-wealth ignited regional interests, ethno-regional consciousness, and created tensions between regional authorities and central government; and third, oil and gas politics is creating governance difficulties leading to violence between government and local communities over the operations of oil companies.

Decisional conflicts arose when key political actors expressed discontent over their limited access to critical oil-linked information (International Crisis Group, 2012b) contrary to provisions for participatory decision-making. Actual decision making violates institutional rights, mandates and obligations, leading to suspicions about the future of heterogeneous Uganda "Despite the great advances towards a multi-ethnic national identity and pluralist political system under NRM leadership, momentum towards building a 'non-sectarian' Uganda has waned" over the years as commentators attack 'Westerners' for dominating Uganda's sociopolitical and economic landscape and the national fragmentation practices evidenced in the ongoing districtisation. International Alert warns that perceptions rumours and concerns regarding the presence of herdsmen, popularly known as *Balaalo,* in the Albertine Graben tend to link these *Balaalo* to national leadership elites and petroleum deposits. This tendency to link the *Balaalo's* occupation of oil-rich areas with political and military elites need not be factual; it can lead to progress from latent to manifest conflicts. Kathman and Shannon predict domestic instability linked to petroleum developments in Uganda, as rapid unplanned urbanization engenders urban crime and insecurity; unpredictability in tax revenue collection and management that may lead to political conflicts; and the formation of rebel groups exploiting grievance over mismanagement of oil and gas revenues or in an attempt to violently take control over petroleum (Kathman and Shannon, 2011). No concrete evidence supports their predictions. But conflict-prone societies like Uganda allow space for such prognosis.

There was *electoral polarisation* during the 2016 general elections as *petroleum* remained at the heart of presidential and parliamentary election campaigns. While many presidential candidates, save for perhaps Amama Mbabazi and incumbent Yoweri Museveni, were not in government and hence uninvolved in developing contracts signed with oil companies (Muhindo, 2016), the 15 January 2016 presidential debate unraveled their interests in the sector. Museveni blamed his electoral opponents of desiring to force him out of office to leave the oil money. Sounding his unwillingness, Museveni stated: "...Then you hear people say 'Museveni should go'. But go and leave oil money? They want me to go so they can come and spoil the oil money. These people want me to go back to the bush" (Kafeero, 2015). This kind of "oil politics" creates competing intrastate interests in securing control over oil and creates electoral fault-lines around the resource (Le Billon, 2010). The candidates, raised oil-related concerns in their campaign rhetoric, and warned the incumbent against corruption in the sector.

Resolving Intra-State Conflicts in Uganda's Oil Sector

Intrastate conflict-resolution mechanisms in Uganda require augmentation through capacity development and institutionalization to avoid short-termism and capacity limitations that (Ramsbotham *et al* (2011) critique. Institutionalization is important because "Societies with institutions, rules or norms for managing conflict and well-established traditions of governance are generally better able to accommodate peacefully to change; those with weaker governance, fragile social bonds and little consensus on values or traditions are more likely to buckle."Institutionalization and coordination are important in managing oil and gas conflicts in the medium to long-term, and exist at different levels and involve multiple stakeholders and actors. Their effectiveness, however, remains limited because they are not tailored to oil conflicts. This adjustment in the focus, locus, and agency of existing conflict management measures ought to be is deliberate, intended to bring these disparate actors into a single institutional fold encompassing both oil and non-oil issues in order to ensure institutionalized and multilevel agency. This vindicates Galtung's notion of institutionalized conflict resolution (Galtung, 1965).

Local level mechanisms involve Local Councils (LCs), faith leaders, cultural leaders and Community Based Organisations (CBOs). Faith and cultural leaders play reconciliatory roles. A key component of community mechanisms, in Uganda's specific context, consists of Local Council (LC) Courts. LCs are the nearest centers for dispute resolution in Uganda's local governance. They range from LC I (village level) to LC V (District level). LCs constitutes Local Council Courts established by an Act of Parliament. LC Courts exist at every village, parish, town, division, and sub-county level, and are composed of all members of the executive committee of the village or parish. At town, division or sub-county levels they comprise "five members appointed by the town council, division council, or sub-county council, on the recommendation of the respective executive committee." in addition, "at least two members of the town, division or sub-county local council court shall be women."Members of LCs, MPs, members of statutory bodies, and members of any other local council courts are barred from being members of specific LC Courts (Republic of Uganda, 2006). It is difficult to demonstrate empirically the intensity, extensity, and variety of cases and instances in which LC courts have handled oil-related conflicts especially involving land compensations. But given the regularity of oil-instigated land conflicts the task is reasonably immense (Republic of Uganda, 2006).

The LC Courts Act provides that "the jurisdiction of a local council court shall extend only to *causes and matters arising within the territorial area of the council* for which the court is established and to *causes and matters arising elsewhere if the defendant or accused is ordinarily resident within that area*" (Sec. 9), and can handle "matters relating to land" and other civil matters [(sec. 10(1) (e)]. Their reliefs include: reconciliation; declaration; compensation; restitution; awarding costs; apology; attachment and sale; and, in the case of infringement of a bye-law or Ordinance, impose fines, community service or any other penalty authorised by that bye-law or Ordinance (Sec. 13). The appeals process of LC courts follows judicial hierarchy to the High Court. These LC Courts are mandated to handle conflicts of varying degrees, though they "shall not order the attachment and sale of the property of an incorporated company unless the company is itself the judgment debtor" (Sec. 28(2)). This legal bar forces LC courts to refer cases involving oil companies to higher courts though the LC courts provide first-stop adjudication in such cases. The main challenge that affects LC courts is that their members were not trained and facilitated to dispense justice, in accordance with the principles of natural justice, customary law, and civil law that are provided for in the LC Courts Act. This challenge has led to ineffectiveness of these courts. In other words, the judiciary remains distanced from the very communities it is [theoretically] mandated to serve.

Religious leaders are important for both spiritual guidance and moral support to the communities. One need not theorize the social function of religion (Ellwood, 1913) to convince the reader about the role played by religious structures in conflict and conflict management if not in Uganda (Jackson, 2009) then elsewhere in Africa and the world: "religion can both encourage conflict and build peace, reflecting growing evidence that religious forces can play a constructive role in helping to resolve conflicts (Haynes, 2009)." People consult religious leaders on mundane but important decisions like buying and selling land. These leaders are sometimes local heroes in their communities and/or opinion leaders that symbolize, or at least create a semblance of, and oftentimes facilitate, unity and reconciliation. Religious leaders' interventions, however, are merely advisory and not legally binding in such matters as oil and gas tensions involving international players. They are not integrated in LC court structures. Non-integration of religious and spiritual leaders in local conflict management structures fragments conflict-resolution mechanisms, which, were they properly coordinated, would handle oil-related conflicts at local level. It would also supplement cultural institutions.

The existence of what are called "cultural/traditional leaders" sometimes fills governance gaps including conflict resolution. These authority structures are remnants of pre-colonial states, but which were overtaken by colonial and post-colonial state-authority structures. Bunyoro-Kitara kingdom has centuries-old centralised authority structures headed by a hereditary royalty with governance structures straddling the whole kingdom. These continuities from pre-colonial to post-colonial governance are potentially useful for countering (or, should need arise, facilitating) ethnic mobilisation against oil companies and government (Moore, 2013). Being rooted in the community's long history of local-level governance and conflict management, kingdom structures have effective mechanisms for detecting and preventing conflicts in their areas of jurisdiction.

However, kingdom structures are not integrated in formal conflict resolution mechanisms. Scholars argue that societies with precolonial centralisation tend to co-exist peacefully with central-state authorities because preexisting control structures are spaces within which central states can negotiate concessions. This interface engenders "civil peace through [a] nonviolent civil bargaining" (Wig, 2013) which may elude societies that were decentralized before colonialism. Wig argues that "strong traditional political institutions facilitate credible nonviolent bargaining between excluded ethnic groups and the state" (Wig, 2013, page 2) thereby reducing these groups' conflict propensity. Unfortunately Bunyoro-Kitara Kingdom has been sidelined. Its proposals and demands regarding sharing revenues and royalties were ignored for long: "the Bunyoro kingdom has called for a greater share of oil revenues as compensation for hosting the oil extraction infrastructure" (Kathman and Shannon, 2011): Inattention to these demands incentivized groups like Bunyoro-Kitara Reparations Agency (BUKITAREPA), to engage in activities that made government concerned about their potential to unfold dangerously and engender national peace and security (Bigiriwenkya, 2016) as Kathman and Shannon prognosticate. While the NOGP appreciates involvement of the kingdom, government did not institutionalize Bunyoro-Kitara's involvement possibly out of fear that other traditional authority structures in non-Bunyoro oil regions would demand the same, thereby creating nationwide demands for indigenizing and/or traditionalizing oil and gas management.

National level judicial, administrative and political measures are intended to resolve disputes basing on written laws and political correctness. The judiciary can resolve conflicts over sharing of royalties basing on the provision that 50 per cent of the revenue from royalties due to Local Governments (LGs) shall be shared among LGs involved in petroleum production based on the level of production of each LG or impact; and that the remaining 50 per cent of the revenue from royalties due to LGs shall be shared among all the LGs "based on population size, geographical area and terrain"('Public Finance Management Act, Sec. 75(3) and 75(4).', 2015). Uganda's judicial system depends on written law and judicial precedence. The judiciary can resolve tax disputes, interpret and enforce contracts, and, in cases of breach of contracts, punish recalcitrance. Recent cases involving Tullow Oil, Heritage Oil, and URA demonstrate the judiciary's role in resolving oil conflicts(*Heritage Oil & Gas Ltd Vs Uganda Revenue Authority (Civil Appeal No 14 Of 2011)*, 2015). Uganda's judiciary, however, suffers delays to deliver judgments, case back-log and numerical inadequacy of judicial officers. The Chief Justice blamed case backlog on lawyers and promised "stringent measures to punish lawyers who do not make adequate preparations prior to court appearances" (Republic of Uganda, 2015a), yet the Justice and Law Reform Sector (JLOS) indicates that case backlog has for long afflicted Uganda (Wolimbwa, no date). Benjamin Odoki reveals that: "inordinate delay in bringing cases to trial and in hearing appeals" hinders administration of justice, results in "a flagrant violation" of the right to fair and timely trial, and is "a serious threat to the quality of justice" (Odoki, 1994) Kaweesa likened *Case Backlog*—"cases that have stayed in the judicial system for two years and beyond"—in Uganda (Kaweesa, 2012) "to the old folklore of the monstrous ogre whose head was overgrown with untidy hair." These limitations hinder the judiciary's reliability in resolving oil and gas conflicts.

There may be other politico-administrative mechanisms. But the last-resort measure for conflict resolution should be examined in relation to previous conflicts in Uganda: ***the military approach***. Military conflicts are conflict-resolution measures to the extent that they are armed contestations intended to resolve the conflict through defeat/capitulation. Since 1972, Uganda has suffered numerous armed conflicts; some interstate, others *transnational*, others *counter-insurgency* operations. The most important and recent are the Joseph Kony-led LRA, and the Jamil Mukulu-led ADF (Titeca and Vlassenroot, 2012) all of which remain weakened but unresolved. Both groups remain scattered in the vast Central African region (United Nations, 2015), and can be potentially re-mobilized, reconstituted, and re-armed to destabilize Uganda. These conflicts operated wholly or in part in areas proximate to the petroleum-rich region. They were mainly addressed using the military approach, involving counterinsurgency operations, as peace talks were hardly fruitful. Developing military, para-military, and intelligence capabilities necessary to counter armed conflicts remains part of Uganda's political-military outlook. Uganda's military, the UPDF, has deployed in the Albertine region to counter such threats (Ssekika, 2009). Not that a military solution is necessarily sufficient for resolving petro-violence, but that military safeguards provide the minimum environment within which peaceful resolution can unfold. Armed confrontations may constitute steps toward resolution when parties resort to "escalation to pursue constructive change" (Ramsbotham *et al.*, 2011). Costly and destructive as war tends to be, a war-less petroleum sector is desirable but hard to predict in conflict-prone Uganda unless deliberate efforts are made toward this outcome.

Three uncomfortable observations arise from a critical examination of the foregoing intra-state conflict resolution measures, relating to: institution; coordination; implementation. On institution, these mechanisms remain scattered in different governance instruments. Implementation structures, such as LC Courts, are not fully equipped, making their capacity and efficacy difficult to evaluate. On coordination, it remains unclear how community-level mechanisms interface with religious and cultural-traditional mechanisms that have for long assisted people to settle disputes. Regarding petroleum-induced migratory tensions, the NOGP "recognizes the need to guide population movements and settlements triggered by oil and gas activities", and prefers local residents in the oil region and promises to limit migrations through distribution of oil-related development and infrastructure (Republic of Uganda, 2013). But no broad conflict-resolution framework integrates these mechanisms or targets oil and gas migrations and conflicts. Likewise, operationalisation of existing mechanisms, especially

LC courts, and interface between Bunyoro-Kitara kingdom and the government, remain haphazard. Military deployments themselves require diplomatic engagement with the DRC to avoid misgivings about border deployments, as well as good civil-military relations to avoid civil-military conflicts. While bilateral measures previously diffused DRC - Uganda tensions, the two neighbours are still unfriendly (Aluma and Okello, 2015) and within Uganda's civil-military landscape tensions remain (Wanambwa and Kasasira, 2013). Filling these policy and technical gaps has vital ramifications for building the country's institutional capacity for multilevel and multi-stakeholder resolution of petroleum-related conflicts.

Conclusion

Pessimism inheres in the resource conflict thesis, which underscores the direct relationship between natural resource endowments, mainly oil and gas, and conflicts within and between states. Scanty attention, however, is paid to mechanisms for resolving conflicts that may afflict nascent oil and gas polities, hence limiting our understanding of the theory and practice of oil-linked conflict resolution. Through qualitative investigate-on, the author analyzed mechanisms for resolving conflicts in Uganda's Albertine Graben underscoring existing conflicts in the Graben and examining extant conflictresolution channels. The cases reveal that existing conflict resolution mechanisms are neither coordinated nor adapted to oil nor gas conflicts. Aware of the potential and actual cross-border/inter-state conflicts, the chapter presented illustrations of intra-state tensions to stress that effective oil-conflicts resolution requires the development, operationalization, and coordination of multilevel conflict-resolution mechanisms. Instituting prior conflict management measures before the sector develops makes it easier to predict, detect, mitigate, de-escalate, and resolve oil and gas conflicts.

Clearly, the Albertine Graben is ripe for both development and struggles as petroleum conflicts change over time. Current tensions in the Albertine Graben are rooted in failure to effectively manage foreign and local pressure to develop the oil and gas sector, land/natural-resource dependence, weaknesses in local and central governance structures, and disruption of traditional livelihoods forcing people to new livelihood challenges without adequate support mechanisms.

Unresolved communal conflicts, clashes between districts and central government, between oil companies and government, between Bunyoro-Kitara kingdom and government, need a solution. Misgivings in the DRC about Uganda pumping Congolese oil underneath Lake Albert feed fears that the 2007 DRC-Uganda border clashes are linked to petroleum (*Uganda/DRC: Museveni and Kabila Discuss Olt and Oil*, 2011). Extant conflict-resolution mechanisms lack institutional coordination and mandate to handle petroleum conflicts, while cross-border conflicts remain unresolved. A fully constituted conflict management strategy is needed to prevent conflict escalation, avoid disruptions arising from lack of coordinated responses to conflicts, and resolve existing conflicts. This caution is useful because oil exploitation process tends to take long, is expensive, demands investments in infrastructure, and affects other sectors of the economy, resource accumulation and wealth distribution within the economy.

Beyond already-experienced tensions, these issues may generate objective grievances and future conflicts over petroleum wealth management. These tensions are not reducible to local struggles but may unfold widely to cross-border and regional levels. Developing and adapting multilevel conflict management measures, in a coordinated manner, should inform policy and research on the nascent oil and gas industry in Africa's Great Lakes Region. While potential broader conflictsover contested borders, Uganda DRC tensions, transboundary pollution, managing transnational structures like the pipeline, destruction of shared ecosystems, and potential pollution of the Nile Waters—can be mitigated through various measures, existing mechanisms ought to be tailored to oil and gas conflicts and accordingly mandated to handle such tensions at different levels. Beyond addressing current intra-state conflicts and preventing new ones, the need for bilateral and regional institutional frameworks for handling petroleum conflicts cannot be overemphasized.

References

Alao, A. (2007) *Natural Resources and Conflict in Africa: The tragedy of Endowment*. New York: University of Rochester Press.

Van Alstine, J., Manyindo, J., Smith, L., Dixon, J. and AmanigaRuhanga, I. (2014) 'Resource governance dynamics: The challenge of "new oil" in Uganda', *Resources Policy*. Elsevier, 40(June), pp. 48–58. Available at: https://doi.org/10.1016/j.resourpol.2014.01.002.

Aluma, C. and Okello, F. W. (2015) 'Tension as DRC is accused of encroaching on border', *Daily Monitor*. Available at: http://www.monitor.co.ug/News/National/Tension-as-DRC-is-accused-of-encroaching-on-border/-/688334/2745872/-/px9mvuz/-/index.html.

Atuhairwe, R. (2012) 'Bunyoro Demands Oil Pre-Production Accountability', *TheNew Vision*.

Bigiriwenkya, A. (2016) 'BUKITAREPA sues Attorney General, Oil Companies for Outrageous oil activities', *GMEPA News*, 24 June. Available at: http://gmepa.com/bukitarepa-sues-attorney-general-oil-companies-for-outrageous-oil-activitiesgmepa-news/.

Le Billon, P. (2010) 'Oil and Armed Conflicts in Africa', *African Geographical Review ISSN:*, 29(1), pp. 63–90. doi: 10.1080/19376812.2010.9756226.

Collier, P. (2003) *Natural Resources, Development and Conflict: Channels of Causation and Policy Interventions*. Oxford: Oxford University & World Bank.

Collier, P., Hoeffler, A. and Rohner, D. (2009) 'Beyond Greed and Grievance: Feasibility and Civil War", *Oxford Economic Papers*, 61, pp. 1–27.

Ellwood, C. A. (1913) 'The Social Function of Religion', *American Journal of Sociology*, 19(3), pp. 289–307.

Fearon, J. and Laitin, D. (2003) 'Ethnicity, Insurgency and Civil War', *The American Political Science Review*, 97(1), pp. 75–90.

Frynas, J. G. and Paulo, M. (2007) 'A New Scramble for African Oil? Historical, Political, and Business Perspectives', *African Affairs*, 106(423), pp. 229–251.

Galtung, J. (1965) 'Institutionalized Conflict Resolution: A Theoretical Paradigm', *Journal of Peace Research*, 2(4), pp. 348–397.

Haynes, J. (2009) 'Conflict, Conflict Resolution and Peace-Building: The Role of Religion in Mozambique, Nigeria and Cambodia', *Commonwealth & Comparative Politics*, 47(1), pp. 52–75.

Heritage Oil & Gas Ltd Vs Uganda Revenue Authority (Civil Appeal No 14 Of 2011) (2015). Uganda.

Humphreys, M. (2005) 'Natural Resources, Conflicts and Conflict Resolution: Uncovering the Mechanisms', *Journal of Conflict Resolution*,

49(4), pp. 508–537.

International Crisis Group (2012a) 'Uganda: No Resolution to Growing Tensions', *Crisis Group Africa Report No.187*.

International Crisis Group (2012b) 'Uganda: No Resolution to Growing Tensions', *Crisis Group Africa Report*. London: ICG, (187), p. 22.

Jackson, P. B. (2009) 'Negotiating with Ghosts': Religion, Conflict and Peace in Northern Uganda', *The Round Table: The Commonwealth Journal of International Affairs*, 98(402), pp. 319–331.

Kafeero, S. (2015) 'Opposition fire back at Museveni over oil control', *Daily Monitor*. Available at: http://www.monitor.co.ug/SpecialReports/Elections/Opposition-fire-back-at-Museveni-over-oil-control/-/859108/3006804/-/xcoqc7z/-/index.html.

Kathman, J. and Shannon, M. (2011) 'Oil Extraction and the Potential for Domestic Instability in Uganda', *African Studies Quarterly*, 12(3), pp. 23–45.

Kaweesa, G. (2012) *Case Backlog and the Right to Due Process: The Uganda Judiciary*. Kampala: Makerere University. Available at: http://www.parliament.go.ug/new/images/stories/jud_backlog.pdf.

Kigambo, G. (2013) 'Oil districts' cause conflict in Uganda', *The East African*, 4 May.

Klare, M. T. and Volman, D. (2006) 'The African "oil rush" and US national security"', *Third World Quarterly*, 27(4), pp. 609–628.

Ladu, I. M. (2015) 'Government wins Heritage Oil case', *Daily Monitor*. Kampala. Available at: http://www.monitor.co.ug/News/National/Government-wins-Heritage-Oil-case/-/688334/2635614/-/gw2sjj/-/index.html.

Ministry of Energy and Mineral Development (2017) 'The National Oil and Gas Policy for Uganda', (February), pp. 1–33.

Moore, A. (2013) *Investigating Causes of Ethnic Identification and Mobilisation in Oil-Rich Regions: Ethnicity, Birthplace, and Revenue Sharing in Bunyoro, Uganda*. Yale: Yale University.

Mugerwa, F. (2014) 'Hoima clashes: Bunyoro Kingdom minister held', *Daily Monitor*, 14 December. Available https://www at:.monitor.co.ug/News/National/Hoima-clashes-Bunyoro-Kingdom-minister-held/688334-2547484-cwubucz/index.html.

Mugerwa, F. and Muzoora, G. (2014) 'Youth question Bunyoro MPs silence on oil', *The New Vision*.Kampala. Available at: http://www.monitor.co.ug/News/National/Youth-question-

Bunyoro-MPs-silence-on-oil/-/688334/2483762/-/7ihe06/-/index.html.

Muhindo, J. (2016) 'Uganda: Oil and gas was tie breaker at presidential debate', *Online: Pambazuka News*. Available at: http://www.pambazuka.net/en/category.php/comment/96528.

Odoki, B. (1994) 'Reducing delay in the administration of justice: The case of Uganda', *Criminal Law Reform*, 5(1), pp. 57–89.

'Public Finance Management Act, Sec. 75(3) and 75(4).' (2015).

Ramsbotham, O., Woodhouse, T. and Miall, H. (2011) *Contemporary Conflict Resolution*. Cambridge: Polity Press.

Republic of Uganda (2006) 'The Local Councils Courts Act'. Entebbe: UPPC (Sections 3-5).

Republic of Uganda (2011a) *The Institution of Traditional or Cultural Leaders Act*. Entebbe: UPPC.

Republic of Uganda (2011b) 'Tullow Oil Vs. Uganda Revenue Authority - TAT Application No. 4 of 2011'. Kampala: Tax Appeals Tribunal/Uganda Legal Information Institute.

Republic of Uganda (2012) *Uganda's Oil and Gas Sector: Many achievements and more are yet to be made*. Kampala.

Republic of Uganda (2013) *The National Oil and Gas Policy (NOGP) for Uganda*. Kampala: MEMD.

Republic of Uganda (2015a) 'Chief Justice Blames Case Backlog on Lawyers'. The Judiciary. Available at: http://www.judicature.go.ug/data/news/173/Chief.

Republic of Uganda (2015b) 'Public Finance Management Act'. Kampala: UPPC.

Republic of Uganda (2015c) 'The Public Finance Management Act', *The Uganda Gazette No. 11 Volume CVIII*. Entebbe: UPPC.

Ross, M. (2003) 'Natural Resources and Civil War: An Overview'. Dept of Political Science: UCLA. Available http://www.unepfi at:.org/fileadmin/documents/conflict/ross_2003.pdf (Accessed: 21 October 2015).

Ross, M. L. (2008) 'Blood Barrels Why Oil Wealth Fuels Conflict By Michael L. Ross From', *Foreign affairs (Council on Foreign Relations)*, 87(3). Available at: https://www.researchgate.net/profile/Michael_Ross11/publication/265273566_Blood_Barrels_Why_Oil_Wealth_Fuels_Conflict/links/56cc7bec08ae1106370d9426/Blood-

Barrels-Why-Oil-Wealth-Fuels-
Conflict.pdf?_sg%5B0%5D=tOwBeAFzwRdnopJjGAAKctyP1JD_
0h5c5algr97p4ceb1tnsfatpnab02_Labrrg7la8jvewaknow9lknex6oa.Vi
np3y0bvyvuieovricaau9zd-
Sd6fhxff9uqemt0fuzcmcc42pnftdgopnfwegxyl49anyvxhgbj_3bkwb3
uw&_Sg%5B1%5D=Dmapfxoun9-
Hzpngy42jy1eyfysq2xykbvumd4lslronkyk4tdzyne4g_DQ2mHEPoC
GPhgvPmchpmCemX2KuHTbqhkrCXL8cPdgSeF8mipTQ.Vinp3y0
bvyvuieovricaau9zd-
Sd6fhxff9uqemt0fuzcmcc42pnftdgopnfwegxyl49anyvxhgbj_3bkwb3
uw&_Iepl=.

Shaxson, N. (2007) *Poisoned Wells: The Dirty Politics Of African Oil.* New York: Palgrave Macmillan.

Ssekika, E. (2009) 'More Land Trouble In Bunyoro As UPDF Seeks To Evict 300: The Army Wants To Build A Military Base On This Land To Protect The OilWells In The Region', *The Observer.* Available At: Http://Www.Observer.Ug/Component/Content/Article?Id=4726:More-Land-Trouble-In-Bunyoro-As-Updf-Seeks-To-Evict-300.

Swanson, P. (2002) *Fuelling Conflict: The Oil Industry And Armed Conflict.* Fato Institute For Applied Social Sciences. Available At: Electronic:

Titeca, K. And Vlassenroot, K. (2012) 'Rebels Without Boarders In Rwenzori Boarderland? A Biography Of The Allied Defence Forces', *Journal Of East African Studies,* 6(1), Pp. 154–176.

Uganda/DRC: Museveni And Kabila Discuss Olt And Oil (2011). Available At: Http://Wikileaks.Ikiru.Ch/Cable/09kampala241/.

United Nations (2014) 'Resolution Adopted By The General Assembly On 10 December 2014 - 69/116', *United Nations Convention On Transparency In Treaty-Based Investor-State Arbitration. Yew York: Un.* Available At: Http://Daccess Dds Ny.Un.Org/Doc/Undoc/Gen /N14/686/64/Pdf/N1468664.Pdf?Openelement.United Nations (2015) *Report Of The Secretary-General On The Implementation Of The Peace, Security And Cooperation Framework For The Democratic Republic Of The Congo And The"Region,"S/2015/735."*New"York:"Unsc. Available"At:"Http://Www.Securitycouncilreport.Org/Atf/Cf/%7b 65bfcf9b-6d27-4e9c-8cd3-Cf6e4ff96ff9%7d/S_2015_735.Pdf.

Wanambwa, R. And Kasasira, R. (2013) 'Probe Assassination Claims, Says Tinyefuza', *Daily Monitor.* Kampala. Available At:

Http://Www.Monitor.Co.Ug/News/National/Probe-Assassination-Claims--Says-Tinye/-/688334/1844358/-/Fjq5ayz/-/Index.Html.

Watts, M. (2001) 'Petro-Violence: Community, Extraction, And Political Ecology Of A Mythic Commodity', In Peluso, N. L. And Watts, M. (Eds) *Violent Environments*. Ithaca And London: Cornell University Press, Pp. 189–212.

Wig, T. (2013) *Peace From The Past: Pre-Colonial Political Institutions And Contemporary Civil Wars In Africa*. Oslo: Peace Research Institute, University Of Oslo.

Wikileaks (2009) 'Museveni Mixes Toxic Brew Of Ethnicity And Oil In Western Uganda'. Kampala: Pol/Econ Chief Aaron Sampson,Embassy Kampala. Available At: Https://Wikileaks.Org/Plusd/Cables/09KAMPALA946_A.Html (Accessed: 8 February 2016).

Wolimbwa, G. P. (No Date) 'The Role Of The JLOS Case Backlog Reduction Programme: Achievements And Lessons Learned'. Kampala: JLOS. Available At: File://C:/Users/Rwengabo/Downl Oads/Case (Accessed: 28 October 2015).

World Bank (2008) 'Managing Oil Revenue In Uganda: A Policy Note', In *OREA Knowledge Series: No. 1. Proceedings Of A National Seminar On Managing Oil Revenue In Uganda, Munyonyo Commonwealth Resort*. Kampala, Uganda.

World Bank (2009) *Deterring Corruption And Improving Governance In Road Construction And Maintenance*.

CHAPTER FIVE

Land Acquisition and Resettlement: Safeguarding Community Livelihoods in Uganda

Russell Rhoads and Onesmus Mugyenyi

Introduction

Since the discovery of commercially viable oil reserves in 2006, Uganda has made the extraction of oil a high national priority. Investments require substantial capital, often relying on foreign-based capitalization and multinational firms constructing facilities and operating them. Permanent land-taking results from the production 'footprint' involving project components. Land acquisition is triggered by government projects for infrastructure, roads and power grids, a planned refinery, pipelines and waste facilities (Joint Venture Partners, 2016). Other triggers for land access are investment and the development of auxiliary services; development has a "multiplier effect" generating businesses and services, and increasing inflationary pressures on services and the land market. Finally, land speculation is on the rise (Murphy *et al.*, 2017).

The land taking debates have spread across the country, fostering passionate engagement on land rights and ownership. Ugandan government is hard pressed to respond in ways that protect the livelihood status of those who occupy lands, not only in the oil development regions, but all across the nation. As a result, government, developers and industry are operating in a context of increased awareness and pressure to better regulate the potential business and social impacts of development. At the same time, investors are in search of guidance to meet high community and national expectations for a prosperous and just development that protects the interests of those local communities directly impacted by development. They seek a standardised and overarching framework to long-term access to land, specific to the development of oil and gas facilities in the Albertine Graben region. This approach requires a partnership with government in developing a framework compliant with both Ugandan legislation and international standards and best practices to safeguard impacted communities against social risks (Joint Venture Partners, 2016).

This chapter describes how ACODE's research and evidence-based studies contribute to an understanding of these trends, revealing gaps between the aims of national policy and how policy unfolds at the on-the-ground level, impacting communities and their livelihoods (Anyuru *et al.*, 2016). Uganda provides an excellent case study for understanding the spillover effects of rapid development and how government and other stakeholders respond to pressures from its citizens and civil society actors - in ways that protect the interests of those local communities directly impacted by development. The chapter sheds light on key findings. First, national legislation/law is conducive to the national context and aligns with international standards. Second, the strategy will likely serve to make land-taking easier and more frequent, while protecting those who are dispossessed of land and livelihood (International Finance Corporation, 2015). Third, the framework will build the capacity of institutions, project practitioners, and local governments to make implementation mechanisms effective. Fourth, the door is open for long-standing issues of "land rights" and land speculation to come to the fore, especially the status of customary tenure as lands are folded into development and the land market. Finally, a democratic space for local communities will open as they are empowered through the entitlements, tools and resources. This space will allow civil society actors to help communities leverage the land taking and resettlement process in order to strengthen livelihoods, food security, and social autonomy.

Land Expropriation and Land Transfer in Uganda

In Uganda, projects in need of land for infrastructure are increasingly located in challenging and sensitive areas, especially in the case of extractives, with a range of impacts on environment and land-connected communities. Unfortunately, in the absence of a national policy outlining a set of principles for land acquisition and resettlement, the benefits of development are often underachieved. Development requires land, and land expropriation displaces people. Each year, development-based land takings globally displace tens of thousands of people. Land takings are largely driven by increased land investments triggered by increased global demand for energy, minerals and oil resources, food and infrastructure development (Cotula *et al.*, 2009). According to Scholte (2005), globalization is a transformation of economic and social space that occurs with the spread of trans-planetary connections between people. In this view, connections are often supra-territorial, connecting flows of goods, labour, media, and finance capital across the boundaries of regions and nation-states (Appadurai, 1996). A driver of globalization, neoliberalism refers to multiple distinct phenomena, from a set of economic policies or development model to an ideology or academic paradigm (Boas and Gans-Morse, 2009). As a set of economic reform policies, free-market liberalization involves actions that eliminate price controls, deregulate capital markets, lower trade barriers, increase privatization and the role of the private sector while reducing state-owned enterprises, contributing to fiscal austerity and curtailing government subsidies (Scholte, 2005). For example, Braedley and Luxton emphasize how economies are designed to unleash and 'liberate' the processes of capital accumulation (Braedley and Luxton, 2010). The magnitude of finance capital funneled into development and the sheer scale development projects was well-documented. Currently the world is experiencing the "biggest investment boom in human history" (Bretton Woods Project, 2015). It is reported that $6-9 trillion annually (8 per cent of global GDP) are devoted to mega dollar projects across the globe, mainly involving public-private partnerships in the energy sector, including the role of the WB Group shifting to large-scale infrastructure projects.

In developing countries, resources and assets are often "outside" the private sector – for example, land in the form of customary tenure or state-owned enterprises and services (D'Costa, 2017). Neoliberal development allows resources and assets to be unleashed, converted and traded in the private sector, which opens new markets for investment, primarily in the reserve of national elites and foreign interests. It is not surprising, then, that the literature is critical of radical free-market strategies in which global inequalities have risen sharply and people become marginalized, dispossessed, and disenfranchised when public resources are privatized and the rural and urban poor incorporated into market economies (Ganti, 2014).

The connection between economic development and land takings in Africa – and in Uganda – can be illustrated by looking at several case studies. For example, the 2011 African Union report "Minerals and Africa's Development" reveals that investments in the extractive sector have risen in recent years with global competition for the region's resources. The region now has the world's highest rates of return on investment, expected to rise to 7 per cent average growth in gross domestic product (GDP) in coming decades. According to Mbataru (2014), the commodity boom has resulted in a doubling of economic output in the past 15 years with six African countries now in the world's top ten fastest growing economies. This boom in investment by governments and investors will accelerate the rate of land transfers across the continent and the accompanying displacement and vulnerability of rural peoples. Within the context of a free-market approach described above, land takings is a growing and worrisome trend, often described in the literature as "land grabbing." According to the FoodFirst Information and Action Network (2010), land grabbing is possession and/or control of a scale of land by lawful or unlawful means for commercial/industrial production, which is disproportionate in size compared to the average land holding in the region. But as Peters explains: "The fact that the land deals are all fairly new in Africa and that many of the acquired land areas are not yet in production means that the effects on access to land, food security and livelihood for rural people are not yet fully known" (Peters, 2013).

In practice, when government and the private sector buy up large tracts of land at home and abroad, they invest in development projects including dams, mining, tourism infrastructure, special economic zones, and land for biofuels and agriculture. But land takings invariably displace local populations; lands are never "idle" or "empty." The fact that 90 percent of rural lands in Sub Saharan Africa are undocumented poses a formidable challenge to land security for local communities (Byamugisha, 2013). In one study on land acquisition in five African countries (Cotula *et al.*, 2009), the authors explain: "concepts such as 'idle' land often reflect an assessment of the *productivity* rather than *existence* of resource uses. These terms are often applied not to unoccupied lands, but to lands used in ways that are not perceived as "productive" by government.

Low-productivity uses may still play a crucial role in local livelihood, food security strategies and land conservation. Even when forced displacements are planned and obvious, it is argued by states and the private sector that subsequent problems affecting Project Affected Persons (PAPs) are the necessary and unavoidable cost of measures to raise the economic level of the majority (Maldonado, 2010). Both of these examples reflect arguments and rationales for a development approach that, we argue, demands the attention to apply standards of implementation to mitigate the social and environmental risks of population displacement (Cernea, 1997).

Land acquisition and involuntary resettlement in Uganda cannot be viewed in isolation from the broader dynamics of globalization and free-market development. In Uganda land takings are largely triggered by infrastructure development for electricity generation and distribution, roads, mineral and petroleum development, agricultural investments, resettlement for both war and environmental refugees, conservation purposes and land speculation. These projects place land acquisition for development projects at the center of current policy for economic development and implementation. For example, the Uganda Investment Authority (UIA) and the Investment Code Act (1991) play a key role in enabling current investor access to land. Projects involving the displacement of population include the five case studies from the ACODE report (see below), as well as projects for hydroelectricity (Isimba and Karuma dams), reforestation plantations (The New Forests Company), and palm oil agribusiness (Lake Victoria islands) (African Business News, 2015). In the mining sector, the government wants to amend 2001 Mining Act so that investors negotiate directly with the government for access to called for by land and avoid negotiating with the landowners as called for by Section 42 of the Mining Act (Bwesigye, 2014). Directly relevant to this study, the oil and gas sector has launched many projects affecting the Lake Albert region in Uganda.

Uganda has turned to extractives and oil development as a high national priority, as evidence by the recent 2016-17 national budget allocations for oil development (Uganda Budget Information, no date). Oil and gas requires substantial capital investments, often relying on foreign-based capitalization and multinational firms constructing facilities and operating them. Several foreign companies have drilled exploratory wells, estimating the reserves at 6.5 billion oil barrels, and the government of Uganda has issued production licenses to several foreign oil companies. Land expropriation is triggered by government projects for infrastructure, roads and power grids, mineral and oil production, including refineries, pipelines and waste facilities. Land taking is also triggered by private investment and the development of auxiliary services; development has a "multiplier effect" generating businesses and services, and increasing inflationary pressures on services and the land market. Land speculation is on the rise. No matter what form it takes, land takings leads to displacement of people from their ancestral lands and homes, loss of property and disruption and or total destruction of livelihoods.

All these demands for land often result in an increased frequency of "crises" of displacements. In Uganda, land has become a critical source of tensions and conflicts in many parts and regions as population grows rapidly, deforestation spreads, and development expands (USAID, 2010). Land does not have to be arable or associated with current agricultural ecologies. As Ferguson explains (Ferguson, 2006), like other extractive industries, oil and gas is characterized by "enclave" development, attracting substantial investment in isolated regions of a country alighting in enclaves that are starkly disconnected from their national societies. Thus, development can be disconnected throughout a country; investment does not "trickle down," but instead leaps over territories and peoples to limited spatial areas of extraction. While it is true that governments talk about "revenue sharing" and "local content," in many ways communities in oil development zones are impacted widely due to costs of living, competition for land and housing, and land speculation for erecting auxiliary industries and services (Deininger *et al.*, 2011).

Two key factors shape the pattern of land acquisition in Uganda: land tenure patterns and land titling. All of these demands for land put pressure on the land security. As most land in Uganda is classified as customary, protections for land rights are weak for the majority of communities, making them vulnerable to dispossession and displacement. The second factor shaping land acquisition is land titling. Patterns of land tenure and titling act as primary constraints to the establishment and growth of oil-related facilities and businesses, but land takings by government has been facilitated nonetheless. However, Ugandan law places limits on the ability of government to compulsorily acquire land. The Constitution (Section 26(2) (a)), the Land Act (1998) and the Land Acquisition Act Cap. 226 (1965) prohibit the government from using compulsory acquisition to promote investment. Thus, a tension exists between Ugandan law and actual investment and land acquisition practices. According to Strickler (2012), "inefficient (and sometimes corrupt) administration of the title registration system reportedly makes it expensive to verify land ownership, which complicates land transfers. The overall low rate of land registration (only some 20 per cent of land is registered) and difficulties of navigating customary tenure systems on unregistered land make it difficult for investors to acquire land."

There is opportunity in Africa to take advantage of the current investment boom, leveraging abundant and highly valuable natural resources with efforts to enforce policies that reduce the risks of dispossessing poor landholders, while ensuring benefit for investors. In short the controversy of 'land grabs' can be turned into development opportunities. But this will require the participation of many players including Pan-African organizations, Africa governments, the private sector, civil society and development partners, depending in large part on political will (Byamugisha, 2013). In our view, the first step for African countries is the formulation among stakeholders of comprehensive reform on land acquisition supported by the standards set by the international development community. The second step is for countries to adopt multi-stakeholder policies by legislation that ensure robust resettlement and livelihood rehabilitation planning for a range of land-taking types.

Case Studies on Land Expropriation and Impacts on Community Livelihood

What are the effects of this vulnerability on the livelihoods of people occupying lands that are targeted for acquisition? The literature is rich in cases of resulting food insecurity. Constraining the use of land can result in the loss of farming capacity, poor health and nutrition, poverty, a shift to wage labor, migration to urban slums, loss of a sense of belonging and community, separation from burial grounds and cultural sites, and the loss of other assets such as firewood, timber, honey, and medicinal herbs, and grazing land for livestock. Vulnerable groups are especially at-risk such as women, children and the elderly (Anseeuw *et al.*, 2012).

What can be done about land takings and uneven resettlement practices, often resulting in loss of livelihood? In 2016, ACODE published a study identifying five cases of land acquisition and resettlement. The purpose of the study was to capture evidenced-based impacts of development on food security and livelihood (Anyuru *et al.*, 2016). The study approach documented the impacts comparatively, generating empirical evidence on-the-ground – and through the perspectives of those directly impacted – the presence or absence of safeguards and mechanisms during resettlement. Our findings revealed insights on the changed livelihoods of affected communities.

The study model is represented in Figure 5.1. This model represents a way to capture development questions and processes in Uganda. For example, national investment priorities for growth and services shape the way land is utilized for development projects (Box #1). Priorities influence a range of different projects that may trigger land acquisition in various ways (Box #2). Though Ugandans occupy these lands as homes, their livelihoods are disrupted, and many are forced to relocate (Box #3). Our findings from data collection in the field were used as evidence of how mechanisms work or do not work, comparing national and international policies and frameworks for involuntary resettlement (Box #4). In the report we concluded with both detailed strategic recommendations and a framework for a national resettlement policy with the aim of impacting the planning environment, investment patterns, and project implementation related to land acquisition and resettlement.

I. National Development	II. Land Acquisition
• What are Ugandan development priorities? • Which sectors are most affected? • How do foreign interests impact development? • What triggers different types of 'land acquisition'?	• What types of land acquisition are taking place in Uganda? • What are typical patterns in the process of land acquisition? • What roles are played by government and the private sector? • How does land acquisition impact resettlment?
III. Community Livelihood	IV. Policy Environment
• How do communities engage in the process of land acquisition? • What are the impacts of land acquisition on access to land, livelihood, and sustainability? • How do the case studies illustrate the intersections between land acquisition and community responses?	• Which existing frameworks guide development with safeguards for land rights and community livelihood? • What framework represents best practices for "balanced" development? • Which policy guidelines and priniples should be put into place in Uganda?

Figure 5.1: Conceptual Model (Developed by the authors)

The case studies were identified as land related and characterized by conflict, in which whole communities were affected by either resettlement or political action and where development and conservation informed the course of conflict. We also chose the cases based on how each reflected gaps in policy and project implementation in the Albertine region of oil development. Additional criteria consisted of representing both planned government land acquisition projects and private land acquisition for auxiliary oil-related development. Regarding the findings from the case studies, we found that land acquisition was triggered in different ways depending on the type of project. For example, the Hoima to Kaiso/Tonya road was a purely public project for the benefit of the public. Similarly, Mpokya eviction was a conservation project and therefore a public interest project. On the other hand, the oil refinery project site and the Bujagali Hydroelectric Power (BHP) project were acquired under public-private partnership arrangements. Finally, the Rwamutonga oil waste management project site was a case of forceful land eviction by a private individual and possible speculator who wanted to take advantage of the development in the oil sector. Of the cases, we chose three projects in which RAPs (Resettlement Action Plans) were put into place as part of social and environmental impact assessments and project planning and implementation.

The "on the ground" findings highlight a number of adverse experiences tied to resettlement (Anyuru et al., 2016). Of the 288 respondents that were interviewed, 41 per cent said they did not like the eviction process, 42 per cent said they lost property, 24 per cent said they suffered from separation from their social networks, and 34 per cent said it disrupted their livelihoods. A third complained about the valuations and the level of compensation they were given, and 21 per cent disliked the way government and third-party private firms (implementing bodies) responded to their circumstances. Others took issue with the roles leaders and politicians played. Many expressed deep concern about the education of their children.

Project Affected Persons: Land Acquisition significantly affected social units (individual family households and villages) as well as the cultural fabric of society and livelihoods. Children are very much a part of the equation in that 92 per cent of the respondents had children in their households. These children are significantly affected as a result of land acquisition processes.

Consultations and Sensitization: An overwhelming 64 per cent of the respondents claimed that they were not consulted in all the case studies under review during the process of land acquisition. Forty-one per cent denied receiving any sensitization. However, 29 per cent of the respondents acknowledge receiving sensitization on the law relating to land acquisition and 46 per cent on their land rights.

Livelihoods: The study notes that 84 per cent of the respondents derived their livelihood from farming. This situation, after involuntary resettle-ment, had changed significantly in that 44 per cent still relied on farming, which was a major concern and worry of the affected households. Many people used the compensation money to start small businesses, pay for school, cancel debts, or simply exhausted the money on petty items. Similar dynamics affected those from the oil refinery case. And even with compensation of land, it took a period of time to regain a footing and stability, especially in the farming. In the Hoima to Kaiso/Tonya Road case, while most people were not relocated, the impacts of the road construction changed access to properties and businesses; for example many complained that the drainage ditch in the road reserve isolated them and their businesses. Overall, the key issues in all the cases were 1) the loss of productive resources, 2) having to survive on insufficient amounts of money to replace income, economic loss, and 3) an absence of livelihood restoration programmes and projects to assist PAPs. Even when those productive assets and resources are renewed (e.g., when finally fully compensated), PAPs are faced with "starting from scratch" and the time it takes for enterprises to yield products and income. In the meantime, this period of living in limbo impacts PAPs and their families, especially women and children.

Coping Strategies: PAPs adopted different coping strategies depending on their circumstances. For those who were forcefully evicted in the case of Rwamutonga and Mpokya, they depended on relief from NGOs and support from the community. The Mpokya group has since settled and are self-sufficient like most rural Ugandans, given the long period of time that they have spent where they were resettled. However, the Rwamutonga community was found to be in a dire situation since their eviction in August 2014, having lost entire farming livelihoods. Most had to resort to casual labour in the neighborhood of their settlement, often exchanging labour for food or money to meet their food and income needs.

For those who were compensated, as in the case of the oil refinery, most PAPs reported that they depended on food from the market in the short term, and this had a significant impact on their economic situation as it dwindled personal savings. For PAPs waiting for resettlement, some had moved to the nearest trading centers where they rented or became squatters. Most reported exchanging labour for food supplies and cash. Some also indicated they reverted to renting pieces of land from others to carry out cultivation for food production.

For social services such as water, education and health, all respondents reported that they coped by travelling long distances in order to access drinking water, and some from open sources with questionable levels of sanitation. With the exception of the group resettled from the oil refinery project, the findings also established that children either had to travel long distances to access schools, while some dropped out as a coping strategy. In the case of health, a number of people had resorted to traditional methods of treatment, or when the situation was life-threatening patients were taken long distances to access services, often via poor access roads.

PAPs also had to cope with integration into host communities where they were resettled. A closer look illustrates the difficulty of anticipating problems with integration and assimilation upon relocation. In the Mpokya case, the eviction victims resettled in Kibaale were welcomed initially, but later as their populations and political influence grew, they faced threats of being evicted again by the indigenous people. In order to cope, the Mpokya settlers sought integration through attendance of church services, participation in funeral activities, being part of self-help groups, as well as strategic participation in local politics.

The Bujagali PAPs who were resettled in Naminya parish faced hostility allegedly because the host community was envious that they had received compensation money. Some of the hostility was manifest in the form of widespread theft by people from the host and neighboring communities, astronomical prices of goods and services, etc. A coping strategy was to report hostility to local authorities or pay local council people bribes/inducements when seeking assistance.

In the case of the oil refinery, PAPs who relocated to neighboring parishes/villages adopted coping strategies focused on mediating prices and costs of living, finding ways to be integrated into the National ID registration processes, and confronting livestock encroachment and theft by the host communities.

In light of the above, the study recommended comprehensive socio-economic, sociocultural and lifestyle studies of affected people in order to develop livelihood "restoration" packages that would minimize negative project impacts especially on the livelihoods. Experience and practice elsewhere offers an array of tools such as agricultural support, livestock packages, small animal/ chicken production, market gardening, business training, and coop and micro-financing organizations, especially for women's groups (Smyth and Steyn, 2015).

Compensation: The findings document cases of extreme delayed compensation of up to 20 years (Mpokya) and no compensation at all (Rwamutonga), as well as contested assessments and valuations of property by PAPs, with pending litigation cases in Courts (Kabaale Oil Refinery and Hoima-Kaiso/Tonya Road). The prominent and most preferred option for resettlement was cash-only compensation. This option allows individuals to duly exercise their rights as in the case of private disposal of property, but is often abused in situations of involuntary resettlement where male household heads upon receiving compensation money, apply it to non-developmental issues. In addition, livelihood status was impacted by the inability to buy productive lands. During delays in timely payment compensation the ensuing development had driven up prices of land in the region of the development project. Therefore, it became almost impossible for PAPs to restore the same acreage of land they previously owned. Other factors impacting on inability to buy land include poor valuation of property, which informed the decision by some PAPs to seek legal redress from courts of law. With little or delayed compensation, especially among PAPs who did not own much property, they were unable to sustain their livelihoods.

These illustrate why governments should follow international standards on a "replacement cost" approach. Compensation is often based on the "fair market value" of land, commonly defined as the amount a willing seller would pay and a willing buyer would accept in an open market ("willing buyer, willing seller"). As explained by Tagliarino, "In countries with robust and functioning land markets, the replacement cost should be roughly equivalent to fair market value, but this is not always the case. Where land markets are weak or non-existent, the fair market value may be less than the replacement cost. In such cases, the 'replacement cost' approach, or a combination of the FMV and replacement cost approach, may be preferable since it focuses more on the amount it would actually take to replace lost assets(Tagliarino, 2017).

A more preferable option is land-based resettlement - restoring the original land size of PAPs and constructing permanent housing in planned environments serviced by roads, electricity, water, schools and health facilities. But this approach was less frequent because of insufficient or false information given to PAPs (e.g. claims of relocation to natural hazarded areas). This was accompanied by insufficient and/or lack of deliberate measures to ensure proper sensitization of PAPs and the lack of mechanisms that safeguard and ensure the enforcement of the rights of PAPs such as independent witness NGOs and appointed Counsel for PAPs.

In fewer cases, there was gross mismanagement of compensation money by those whose conditions had deteriorated. Some were noted to have spent most of their money on alcohol and less productive activities including taking more women for wives, gambling and acquisition of assets that were less productive such as cars, music systems, etc. There were poor business choices made by some individuals.

Finally, the most negatively impacted persons were from the two forceful evictions. In the Mpokya case, partial compensation took place many years after relocation to Kibaale District, and in 2015 the compensation process was renewed but has yet to be completed. Finally, Rwamutonga represents a case in which no compensation was either planned or awarded. However, in 2016, court decisions handed down in favor of the evictees has resulted in a subsequent court action based on an appeal for compensation and hardship restitution.

The Mpokya evictions happened in 1992; though PAPs have since been resettled, they haven't been fully compensated. The recent eviction at Rwamutonga was also negative in impact. The evicted population have been living in squalid conditions since they were evicted in the second half of 2014 with very little subsistence assistance to help them live a meaningful life. This particular group lost nearly every material possession, including providing for education, health and the feeding of their children due to loss of livelihood.

In summary, we concluded that the existing policy and implementtation for land acquisition in Uganda is uneven and inadequate for safeguarding the rights of PAPs. We saw that the World Bank-sponsored Bujagali dam project was less problematic than the other cases due to the strong social and environmental safeguards built into the planning and implementation process. While some safeguards fell short, grievances were addressed as indicated by the WB Inspection Panel report from 2008. But in the other four cases, the findings demonstrate the overwhelming negative impacts on PAPs and communities at the level of implementation. Laws and policies need to guide the adoption of principles and mechanisms suited to each case at the level of implementation. A robust action plan that provides checks and balances on how the mechanisms are applied will positively impact on lives and status of PAPs, and mitigate such negative consequences as documented in the ACODE study. Communities require significant capacity-building before they can meaningfully participate equitably in projects and be able to make decisions on the restoration of their livelihood. Indeed, land acquisition and restriction on land use often necessitates that people lose agricultural land and businesses, access to natural resources, and social networks. The challenge is not to try and restore pre-existing standards of living (pre-existing poverty?), but rather to improve livelihood through intentional economic strategies (e.g., livelihood restoration) that are built into project planning and implementation. Projects should benefit communities in ways that guarantee economic opportunity and social welfare into the future.

Therefore, it follows that mechanisms for engaging communities during the project planning and implementation (e.g. fair compensation, valuation of property, sensitization, monitoring, and grievance procedures) must be integrated into policy frameworks in both planning and implementation. We acknowledge that the government of Uganda has taken strides towards these ends, most notably integrating the World Bank-influenced Resettlement Action Plans (RAP) into three of the projects we investigated: the oil refinery, the roads project, and the Bujagali hydroelectric power project (Kato, 2014). Even as the RAP-based projects represent progress towards the enforcement of rights by PAPs, more is needed to establish long-term solutions to safeguarding land rights and the welfare of PAPs, guided by a consistent and transparent government policy for resettlement.

This issue connects to the second goal of the research study – to propose principles and mechanisms for a national resettlement policy framework suited to the Ugandan context. The proposed policy would drawfrom the existing national policies, international best practices, and lessons learned from the on-the-ground case studies making up this study. To meet these objectives, the research team reviewed and synthesized the regulatory tools used to ensure social safeguards were adequately managed and taken into consideration. We conducted a "gap analysis" of relevant national Ugandan policies in relation to corporate standards and international 'soft law' guidelines for development, such as the World Bank Operational Policy on resettlement, the International Finance Corporation's (IFC) Performance Standards for Land Acquisition and Involuntary Resettlement, and industry standards, such as the International Petroleum Industry Environmental and Conservation Association (IPIECA) (World Bank, 2016).

The framework developed by ACODE points to what needs enforcing: weak mechanisms, inefficient processes, absence of monitoring, and harmful engagements with project-affected communities. In the next section, we turn to recent innovations to development a national land acquisition and resettlement policy. An analysis of the partnership between government and industry is presented. The proposed framework disclosed by the government/industry partnership reveals a land-taking model that is investor-friendly environment, provides for standardization and long-term stability, and reduces challenges and bottlenecks causing costly delays. At the same time, it aligns with a commitment to policies and practices that can guide resettlement to reduce social and environmental risks.

Government/Industry Initiatives to Development of a Policy Framework for the Oil Sector

The ACODE study paralleled an initiative by industry to develop its own land acquisition and resettlement framework or LARF (Joint Venture Partners, 2016). The framework is a combined effort by three "joint venture partner (JVP) oil firms and The Ministry of Energy and Mineral Development (MEMD) that will govern resettlement activities related oil projects. The goal is to provide an overarching policy framework for the development of upstream oil and gas facilities in the Albertine Graben. The LARF implicitly promotes an investor-friendly environment, secures long-term stability, and reduces the challenges of bottlenecks and delays, such as land conflict and grievance actions in courts of law. The objectives of the LARF are to: (i) define and standardize terminology, objectives, policies, principles and organizational arrangements, (ii) align Ugandan laws and legal requirements to the International Finance Corporation's (IFC) standards for resettlement while respecting national laws and narratives of sovereignty and (iii) provide practical guidance to project personnel (including JV Partners, contractors and consultants) in the planning and implementation (Joint Venture, 2016). Partners, 2016)

One of the key findings of the ACODE study is the disconnect that exists between the legal protection of the rights of individuals to land and livelihood, the attendant rights for compensation as provided in policy and legislation, and the actual realisation of the rights in the course of implementing government development projects. While the World Bank safeguard policies and International Finance Corporation Performance Standards specify procedures when resettlement takes place, these are not always followed effectively. Governments tend to rely on eminent domain resulting in people made worse off as a result of these projects. This is partly because there is limited experience and capacity in good practice resettlement and in social impact assessment (Vanclay, 2017).

The LARF aims to harmonize these national and international standards that mitigate the social impacts of land acquisition and involuntary resettlement (Anyuru *et al.*, 2016). In addition, the LARF requires the development of resettlement action plans (RAP) for each project. The RAP is a planned process of the acquisition of land for projects and/or the physical displacement of people from one place to another, and for the rehabilitation of livelihood, including the restoration and improvement of the living standards and conditions of people affected by resettlement.

In our view, the MEMD's endorsement of the LARF and its application of the IFC standards is a key milestone for moving international best practices one step closer to national law (International Finance Corporation, 2012b). Both the World Bank and IFC frameworks standards go beyond national laws and legislation in providing rights holders with tangible mechanisms sensitive to land acquisition and involuntary resettlement (International Finance Corporation, 2012a).

In the short term, such standards will structure the resettlement process on projects involving petroleum extraction and infrastructure. If implemented as required, the RAPs have the potential of integrating key social safeguard mechanisms. Compensation as envisaged in the RAP must be at full replacement cost for land and other assets lost. Where people living in the project area are required to move to another location, the displaced must as of right be offered choices on feasible resettlement options, including adequate replacement housing or cash compensation where appropriate. In all such cases of displacement, provisions for assistance during relocation suited to the needs of each group of displaced persons must be made. New resettlement sites built for displaced persons must offer improved living conditions.

In addition, the IFC standards require five elements:

Compensation: In every case of compensation there must be transparency, consistency in application to all persons affected. In situations where livelihoods of displaced persons are land-based, displaced persons must be offered land-based compensation. In all cases, possession of acquired land and related assets should be taken only *after* compensation has been made available. Resettlement sites and moving allowances must be provided to the displaced persons in addition to compensation.

Community Engagement: The developer is required to ensure there is active community participation as set out in IFC Performance Standard #1 (International Finance Corporation, 2012b).

Grievance Mechanism: In all situations where involuntary resettlement arises there must be established a grievance handling mechanism and this mechanism must be consistent with the grievance mechanisms set out in IFC Performance Standard 1.

Livelihood Restoration Planning and Implementation: There must be collection of appropriate socio-economic baseline data to identify the persons who will be displaced by a project and to determine who will be eligible for compensation and assistance. Projects must establish procedures necessary to monitor and evaluate the implementation of a RAP or Livelihood Restoration Plan (LRP) and take corrective action as necessary (International Finance Corporation, 2012b).
Certainly, the LARF initiative will add the "teeth" of mandate and enforcement, and the framework provides valuable guidelines and checklists for project implementation.

The LARF represents a land-based approach to restoring livelihood, including recognizing the "informal rights" of *bone fide* occupants (Principle 9 p.10). The approach is especially strong on mitigating loss of livelihood and livelihood restoration, recognized that, "Land-based livelihood improvement opportunities have not been widely tested in Uganda. There is a significant need for appropriate baseline information to plan livelihood restoration activities" (Joint Venture Partners, 2016). While information on farming is central, multiple livelihood strategies (reliance on crops, fishing, livestock, small business, employee, rental incomes, and natural resources) are often equally as important. According to this "integrated approach" strategy, participatory planning is necessary to determine how people rely on land-based and multiple livelihood strategies "to maximize food production and cash generating opportunities and to spread the risk often associated with subsistence livelihoods" (Joint Venture Partners, 2016). Further, the LARF puts into place a provision that "livelihood planning will be based on appropriate technological solutions and technical advice from Government, development NGOs, local consultants, and research and academic institutions" (Joint Venture Partners, 2016). Additional mechanisms for grievance and its monitoring and evaluation are particularly detailed with guiding procedures. Finally, the LARF provides ample engagement with the local and impacted communities at key leverage points in the resettlement planning and implementation process, seeking a positive relationship with the community for negotiating solutions that do no harm to the local population and that reduce social risk" (Joint Venture Partners, 2016). For example, the process relies on community members represented on a Resettlement Committee; compensation signing witnessed by local representatives; and PAP feedback on monitoring activities through "Resettlement Village Committees" and "Resettlement Advisory Group" (Joint Venture Partners, 2016).

One of the challenges of the "integrated approach" is to integrate multiple stakeholders at the community level in a social responsible manner. Where the resettlement process excludes community welfare, such to save time and money, "the risk is that disagreements will arise later which will result in costly delays," undermining the implementation of the project (Smyth and Steyn, 2015). This is why we argue that local communities will require partnerships with civil society (CBOs and NGOs) to rethink and transform development towards inclusive growth that respects social license, community participation and sustainability (Hanna *et al.*, 2016). At the core of this process, 'social accountability' constitutes the rights and duties that exist between people, government, the private sector, and civil society to establish social compacts that share development benefits in society (Khoday and Perch, 2012). For example, an integrated approach will involve coordinated roles by a range of stakeholders – all contributing to project outcomes. The Oxfam publication *Land and Power* describes such roles forcivil society organizations as community capacity-builders (sensitization and consultation) and as monitors of service delivery and accountability mechanisms, such as grievance redress processes (Zagema, 2011). In addition, civil society can be integrated on several project teams involving community consultation, legal advice, financial planning, livelihood programs, baseline and data surveys and monitoring and evaluation. In particular, monitoring and evaluation (M&E) is an internationally and nationally recommended practice. It serves to ensure that what is undertaken to be done within a specified time for a particular community is effectively and promptly done within the specified time frames and is delivered in the terms undertaken (International Finance Corporation, 2012b).

While supporting impacted communities is paramount, practitioners also require capacity building. Practitioners are those experts, bureaucrats and technicians responsible for carrying out projects and following RAP procedures. We acknowledge that legislation and policy often have more to say about what needs to be done, but not much about how it should be planned and actually undertaken. Therefore, the capacity-building for any resettlement project should be complimented with the nuts-and-bolts and "how-to" tools as a practical guide on planning and implementing development "on the ground." NGOs and civil society can play an important training role. Training tools must speak the 'language of the practitioner,' explaining the safeguard mechanisms in simple yet effective terms and capturing the perspectives of stakeholders in order to facilitate communication. One such tool is the people-centered, "well-being" approach to resettlement developed as the "Social Frameworks for Projects" model (Smyth and Vanclay, 2017).

Conclusion

Too often our understanding of land and livelihood is clouded by the use of inappropriate models. As Lindsay, Deininger and Hilhorst argue:

> The legacy of models from countries with developed land markets and vastly different cultural and economic conditions has resulted in legal frameworks that are poorly aligned with the actual contours of land relations in developing countries, and poorly equipped to address the livelihood impacts and governance challenges associated with land taking .... Recent years have seen the emergence of important efforts to break free of this legacy at national levels, and an international convergence of common standards (Lindsay et al., 2017).

But a study by Tagliarino, which assessed the laws of 50 countries against indicators from 2012 Voluntary Guidelines on the Responsible Governance of Tenure of Land (VGGT), found that more than half the countries did not have legal provisions for fair compensation that meet international standards. He recommends that,"robust compensation procedures established by law, coupled with respect for the rule of law, can help ensure that expropriations promote sustainable development outcomes that balance property rights with public interest" (Tagliarino, 2017). Clearly, there is major need for a legislative shift in Uganda and elsewhere where policies and priorities can be put into place that reflect unique national contexts.

One key response for responsible governance is the establishment of a national land acquisition and resettlement policy to try to standardize an overarching framework for land taking – a framework compliant with both Ugandan legislation and international standards and best practices to safeguard impacted communities against social risks. Uganda has moved in this direction with efforts to development a national "land acquisition, resettlement and rehabilitation policy" (LARRP). An innovative step forward, this public/private strategy seeks to promote resource development in conjunction with avoiding project-impacted social risks. The LARRP is a work-in-progress, building upon the LARF policy as described above a policy endorsed by government/JVPs for the oil-producing region. As proposed, the new policy would expand the framework across Uganda and cover projects of land acquisition, involuntary resettlement and rehabilitation, as well as displacement for the purposes of conservation and preservation of the natural environment (forestry, wildlife and wetlands), natural and man-made disasters such as flooding, global climate change, violent conflicts and civil strife (IDPs and refugees). Notably, the policy also applies to cases where government needs land for investment and the constitution does not permit use of compulsory acquisition powers (Uganda Investment Authority and public-private partnerships [PPP]).

Three potential benefits of the Ugandan framework are evident. First, it creates an investor-friendly climate because it sets in place a concrete government-supported framework with predictable and concrete processes allowing for the security of investment. It also serves as a way for the government to bridge gaps in national laws and to indirectly address (or circumvent) sensitive development debates (e.g., land rights, speculation, informal tenure, and PAP livelihood), by integrating the conventions of international best practices for project planning and implementation. Second, it puts an equal emphasis on land acquisition, resettlement, and rehabilitation. From a stakeholder point of view, the model builds mechanisms that integrate and accommodate different livelihood interests. Third, it represents a shift in —the ownership of development as the government develops its own framework with direct ties to international best practices yet aligning this with existing national policies and laws suited to the Ugandan context and narratives of national sovereignty.

Can one expect that social safeguards will be implemented in a more consistent way, applied to a broad range of projects? Will safeguards and restoration of livelihood become accepted as part of the costs and "culture" of doing development? Clearly many challenges remain, such as how the policy framework defines the types and scale of land-taking that trigger application of the policy. Will the policy apply beyond government-sanctioned projects and cases of right of way and eminent domain? Will private investments that result in land taking and the displacement of people serve as a trigger?

While the framework will serve to make land-taking easier and more frequent, it must go further, doing more for those who are dispossessed of land and livelihood (International Crisis Group, 2012). First, "best practice" safeguards to avoid social and environmental risks need to be understood as a key component of the "cost" any development project and land-taking. Second, implementing the policy will require building the capacity of institutions, project practitioners, and local governments to make good on implementation mechanisms that effectively reduce risks and improve the livelihood of impacted communities. Third, the issue of "land rights" and land speculation will remain challenging as lands are opened up to development, converted from customary and leasehold, and folded into development and the land market. Finally, local communities must be fully engaged from the start to finish, provided with the entitlements, tools and guides that allow them resources to leverage the resettlement process on their behalf, in order to strengthen their livelihoods, food security, and social autonomy. ACODE's work contributes to these efforts with evidence-based studies that reveal gaps between the aims of national policy and how policy unfolds at the on-the-ground level, impacting communities and their livelihoods. We seek an approach that "balances development" accounting for the needs of citizens, developers and industry and national Ugandan development priorities.

References

African Business News (2015) 'Uganda's parliament agrees on US$1.44bn loan for Karuma dam'. Available at: http://lankainformation.lk/2015-03-04-04-29-46/african-business-news/item/1006-uganda-s-parliament-agrees-on-us-1-44bn-loan-for-karuma-dam.

Anseeuw, W., Wily, L. A., Cotula, L. and Taylor, M. (2012) 'Land Rights and the Rush for Land: Findings of the Global Commercial Pressures on Land Research Project'. Rome: ILC. Available at: http://www.landcoalition.org/sites/default/files/documents/resources/ILC.

Anyuru, M. A., Rhoads, R., Mugyeni, O., Manoba, J. A. and Balemesa, T. (2016) 'Balancing Development and Community Livelihoods: A Framework for Land Acquisition and Resettlement in Uganda', *ACODE Policy Research SeriesPolicy Research Series*. Environmental Democracy Programme, No. 75. Available at: http://www.acode-u.org /Files/Publications/PRS_75.pdf.

Appadurai, A. (1996) *Modernity At Large: Cultural Dimensions of Globalization*. University of Minnesota Press.

Boas, T. C. and Gans-Morse, J. (2009) 'Neoliberalism: From New Liberal Philosophy To Anti-Liberal Slogan', *Studies in Comparative International Development*, 44(2), pp. 137–161.

Braedley, S. and Luxton, M. (eds) (2010) *Neoliberalism and Everyday Life*. McGill-Queen's Press-MQUP.

Bretton Woods Project (2015) 'The World Bank: In The Vanguard of an Infrastructure Boom', *Bretton Woods Observer*. Winter. Available at: http://www.brettonwoodsproject.org/2015/02/world-bank-vanguard-infrastructure-boom/.

Bwesigye, D. B. (2014) 'Negotiate with Mineral-Rich Land Owners', *Oil in Uganda*. Available at: http://www.oilinuganda.org /features/land/negotiate-with-mineral-rich-land-owners.html.

Byamugisha, F. . F. . (2013) 'Securing Africa's Land For Shared Prosperity: A Program to Scale-Up Reforms and Investments',

International Bank for Reconstruction and Development. Washington D. C: World Bank Publications. Available at: https://openknowledge.worldbank.org/bitstream/handle/10986/13837/780850PUB0EPI00LIC00pubdate05024013.pdf?sequence=1.

Cernea, M. M. (1997) 'The risks and reconstruction model for resettling displaced populations', *World Development*, 25, pp. 1569–1587.

Cotula, L., Vermeulen, S., Leonard, R. and Keeley, J. (2009) *Land Grab or Development Opportunity; Agricultural Investments and International Land Deals in Africa*. London/Rome: IIED/FAO/IFAD.

D'Costa, A. P. (2017) 'Land, Livelihoods, and Late Capitalist Development', *The Land Question in India: State, Dispossession, and Capitalist Transition*, p. 325.

Deininger, K., Byerlee, D., Lindsay, J., Norton, A., Selod, H. and Stickler, M. (2011) *Rising Global Interest in Farmland: Can It Yield Sustainable and Equitable Benefits?* Washington DC: The World Bank.

Ferguson, J. (2006) *Global Shadows: Africa in the Neoliberal World Order*. Duke University Press.

FoodFirst Information and Action Network (2010) *Annual report 2010*. Heidelberg, Germany: FAIN International. Available at: http://www.fian.org/library/publication/detail/fian_annual_report_2010/.

Ganti, T. (2014) 'Neoliberalism', *Annual Review of Anthropology*, 23(1), p. 92.

Hanna, P., Vanclay, F., Langdon, E. J. and Arts, J. (2016) 'Conceptualizing Social Protest and the Significance of Protest Actions to Large Projects', in *The Extractive Industries and Society 3*, pp. 217–239.

International Crisis Group (2012) 'Uganda: No Resolution to Growing Tensions', *Crisis Group Africa Report*. London: ICG, (187), p. 22.

International Finance Corporation (2012a) 'IFC Sustainability Framework', *Policy and Performance Standards on Environmental and Social Sustainability*, (Performance Standard No. 5). Available at: http://www.ifc.org/wps/wcm/connect/topics_ext_content/ifc_external_corporate_site/ifc+sustainability/our+approach/risk+management/performance+standards/environmental+and+social+performance+standards+and+guidance+notes.

International Finance Corporation (2012b) 'Policy and Performance Standards on Environmental and Social Sustainability'. Available at:

http://www.ifc.org/wps/wcm/connect/topics_ext_content/ifc_external_corporate_site/ifc+sustainability/our+approach/risk+management/performance+standards/environmental+and+social+performance+standards+and+guidance+notes.

International Finance Corporation (2015) *The Art and Science of Benefit Sharing in the Natural Resource Sector*. Washington, DC: International Finance Corporation.

Joint Venture Partners (2016) 'Land Acquisition and Resettlement Framework (LARF): Petroleum Development and Production in the Albertine Graben'. Kampala: project components, pp. 14–16. Available at: http://ug.total.com/en/land-acquisition-and-resettlement-process (Accessed: 16 May 2017).

Kato, T. (2014) *Rap Implementation and Land Acquisition for Development in the Albertine Region: A Case Study of Buseruka Sub County, Kabaale Parish, Hoima District*.

Khoday, K. and Perch, L. (2012) *Development From Below: Social Accountability in Natural Resource Management*. International Policy Centre for Inclusive Growth.

Lindsay, J., Deininger, K. and Hilhorst, T. (2017) 'Compulsory Land Acquisition in Developing Countries: Shifting Paradigm or Entrenched Legacy?', in Kim, I., Lee, H., and Somin, I. (eds) *Eminent Domain: A Comparative Perspective*. Cambridge University Press, pp. 118–154.

Maldonado, J. K. (2010) 'New Path Forward: Researching and Reflecting on Forced Displacement and Resettlement', *Journal of Refugee Studies*. The Hague, 36.

Mbataru, P. (2014) 'Scramble for Africa Threatens to Leave Continent Starving', m*The Africa Review*. Available at: http://www.africareview.com/Special-Reports/Scramble-for-Africa-threatens-to-leave-continent-starving/-/979182/2225618/-/uii9niz/-/index.html.

Murphy, S., Carmody, P. and Okawakol, J. (2017) 'When Rights Collide: Land Grabbing, Force and Injustice In Uganda', *The Journal of Peasant Studies*, 44(3).

Peters, P. E. (2013) 'Conflicts Over Land and Threats to Customary Tenure In Africa', *African Affairs*, 47, p. 560.

Scholte, A. J. (2005) *The Sources of Neoliberal Globalization*. United Nations

Research Institute for Social Development (UNRISD).

Smyth, E. and Steyn, M. (2015) *Land Access and Resettlement: A Guide To Best Practice*. Greenleaf Publishing.

Smyth, E. and Vanclay, F. (2017) 'The Social Framework For Projects: A Conceptual But Practical Model to Assist in Assessing, Planning and Managing the Social Impacts of Projects', *Impact Assessment and Project Appraisal*, 35(1), pp. 65-80. Available at: https://www.tand fonline.com/doi/abs/10.1080/14615517.2016.1271539.

Strickler, M. (2012) *Governance of Large-Scale Land Acquisitions in Uganda: The Role Of The Uganda Investment Authority*. World Resources Institute, African Biodiversity Collaborative Group (ABCG). Available at: http://www.abcg.org/document_details?document_id=142.

Tagliarino, N. K. (2017) 'The Status of National Legal Frameworks for Valuing Compensation for Expropriated Land: An Analysis of Whether National Laws in 50 Countries/Regions across Asia, Africa, and Latin America Comply with International Standards on Compensation Valuation', *Land*, 6, p. 2.

Uganda Budget Information (no date) 'Ministry of finance Planning and Economic Development'. Available at: http://budget.go.ug /budget/national-budgets-documents.

USAID (2010) *Country Profile Property Rights & Resource Governance: Uganda*. Washington DC: USAID. Available at: https://www.land- links.org /country-profile/uganda-2/.

Vanclay, F. (2017) 'Project-Induced Displacement and Resettlement: From Impoverishment Risks to An Opportunity for Development?', *Impact Assessment and Project Appraisal*, 35(1), pp. 3–21. Available at: http://dx.doi.org/10.1080 /14615517.2017.1278671.

World Bank (2016) *Environmental and Social Standard 5 Land Acquisition, Restrictions on Land Use and Involuntary Resettlement (ESS5)*. Washington, DC, USA: World Bank. Available at: http://www.ifc.org/wps/wcm /connect/topics_ext_content/ifc_external_corporate_site/ifc+sustaina bility/our+approach/risk+management/performance+standards/envir onmental+and+social+performance+standards+and+guidance+notes.

Zagema, B. (2011) 'Land and Power: The Growing Scandal Surrounding the New Wave of Investments in Land', *Oxfam Policy and Practice: Agriculture, Food and Land*, 11(6), pp. 114–164.

CHAPTER SIX

Fish Product Chain: The Case of Lake George in Uganda

Wilson Winstons Muhwezi and Boaz Blackie Keizire

Introduction

In spite of sustaining a relatively high economic growth, the booming fish sector in Uganda has never translated into better standards of living for fishery-dependent communities. An increase in fish products' trade was found to have an invisible impact on fishing communities (MAAIF, 2011). Important to note is the fact that, high Gross Domestic Product (GDP) growth rates in Uganda are not yet synonymous with improved well-being of most people. It is also known that sustainable and stable growth rates in Uganda were found to be associated with environmental and natural resource degradation, estimated to be about 17 per cent of annual Gross National Product (GNP) (NEMA, 2004). Unsustainable exploitation of natural resources directly affects the poor, whose livelihoods entirely depend on natural resources like fish. The introduction of Beach Management Units (BMUs) through legislation in Uganda carried a promise of reducing levels of poverty in fishing communities because it was meant to lead to better management of the resource ('Fish (Beach Management) Rules', 2003). Unfortunately, fish-dependent communities remain relatively poor in spite of all efforts to integrate them in planning for their resource. It is therefore of overarching interest to analyse why fishing communities remain poor, in spite of having access to wealth in the fishery resource.

In a purely political economy analysis, it is fathomable that investments to increase the economic value of natural resources, like fish might not lead to poverty eradication. The poor rarely benefit from commercial exploitation of natural resources. Instead, profit from such a natural resource is extracted and concentrated in the hands of a few powerful intermediaries such as traders, transporters, 'tenderers', and/or state agents. The remaining spoils are divided among private commercial actors and government as profit, taxes, fees, fines and unofficial patronages or gifts along the path from extraction to end use.

This chapter attests to the fact that behaviour patterns among actors in the fish product chain largely account for the marginal economic gains achieved in over forty years of conservation and at least almost a decade of poverty eradication-related planning in Uganda. Using Lake George in South-western Uganda as a case study and while drawing parallels from selected fish-dependent communities on Lake Victoria, extensive fieldwork for this write-up was undertaken between March and April, 2006. The crux of our argument is that interventions that never take cognisance of the nature, power and wealth relations over any resource as well as behavioural characteristics of main actors, always have a dismal impact on society.

This chapter describes the main actors in the fish production and marketing chain, determines the income gains and/or losses that accrue to different actors in the fish production chain, and proposes appropriate responses using Lake George in Uganda as an example. It is based on research and analysis undertaken to trace dynamics that underpin the rationale that explains why fishing communities remain the poorest in spite of having a steady income from fish.

The economic value of fish in Uganda is undisputed. The economic value reached record levels in 2005 when fish exports fetched US $ 143 million, approximating 20 per cent of total exports (MAAIF, 2011). Over the same period, the structure and scope of actors in the fisheries sub-sector underwent significant transformation, epitomized by the increasing dominance of fish processing firms and intermediary operators. Actors like transporters and middle-class business people aggressively joined fish trade. Proliferation into the fish business by hitherto non-fishing actors made fishing an enviable activity. Increasingly, the fisheries sub-sector started to be viewed as a potential growth subsector by Government, since its potential to contribute to GDP and reduce poverty in fishery-dependent communities became more apparent *(The Poverty Eradication Action Plan (PEAP)*, 2004).

Evidence from the fisheries subsector indicated that in spite of the profitable nature associated with fishing, many fish-dependent communities continued to be mired in relative and absolute poverty

(Keizire, 2003). The quality of life in such communities' remained considerably low characterised by low education and poor health indicators. For instance, HIV/AIDS prevalence in such communities was high in fishing villages (3-5 per cent higher than the national average) (Tanzarn and Bishop-Sambrook, 2003). A probable explanation for such trends could be the overemphasis on fishing conservation without corresponding emphasis on the relationship between fishing, power held by each of the actors and wealth derived from the resource. Success in conservation of fish as a resource and poverty eradication among beneficiary communities depends on how policy makers and implementers balance the delicate and complex relationship between the three pillars.

The Nature Wealth and Power (NWP) analytical framework sheds considerable light on these issues. This framework was used to explain why many community development interventions in many African countries fail to produce sustainable results in the area of natural resources conservation(USAID and Africa Bureau (AFR/SD), 2002)(USAID and Africa Bureau (AFR/SD), 2002). This paradox is epitomised by an attempt to ensure the ecological integrity of the environment and natural resources, while improving the socio-economic conditions of targeted communities. Natural resources like fish are a major source of wealth and power and are key to rural development and good governance. The NWP framework analyses the relationship between environmental management, economic concerns and good governance. The framework was widely used in Namibia, Madagascar and Mali. The framework recognises that the natural, economic and governance dimensions of resources is critical to developing appropriate management systems.

The importance of lakes like George in Uganda to the livelihoods of people goes without question. Fish from lakes is a governance issue, especially for lake-dependent communities. Lakes with fish provide an important source of livelihoods, particularly for people involved in fishing and is a source of Government revenue. The range of uses of lakes and associated rivers include water for domestic and industrial use as well as wetlands for seasonal fishing, purification of water coming into the lake, papyrus and sustaining wildlife and fishing. Over 50 per cent of people inhabiting fish landing sites depend on fishing as a primary source of income.

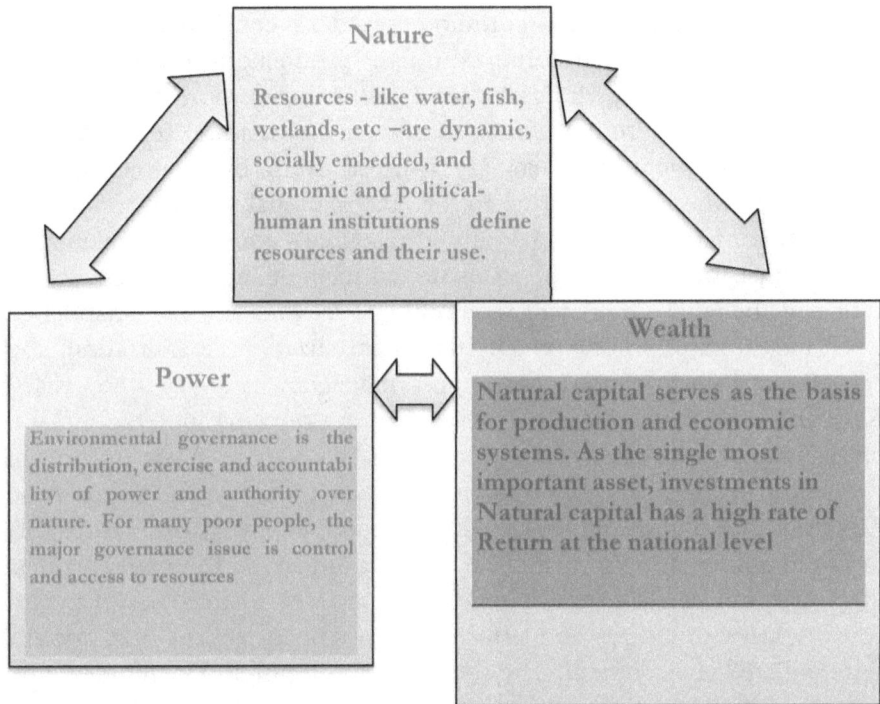

Figure 6.1: Illustration of NWP Framework
Source: (USAID and Africa Bureau (AFR/SD), 2002)

Theoretically, NWP framework as well as the Commodity Chain Analysis (CCA) (Raikes, Jensen and Ponte, 2000) informs the conceptualisation of this chapter. On the nature axis of NWP, the concern is not only the physical make-up of the resource, but also the information and knowledge systems and their management that are critical for sound natural resources management. On the other hand, the wealth axis is about the strategic decisions on economics of natural resource management. It entails an attempt to understand the fish market and reasons for observed poverty in spite of fish-related wealth. Lastly, the power axis looks at understanding the power structures that govern fishing around the resource in an attempt to understand how power relations affect benefit sharing among different actors.

On the other hand, the CCA involves a series of interlinked exchanges through which a commodity and its constituent parts pass (from extraction or harvesting through production, transformation, transport, distribution, wholesale, retail and end use). Commodity chains serve as conduits through which commercialised natural resources like fish and constituent products are ushered from the source to final consumers, whether rural, urban or 'international' (FAO, 2000). By tracing the interactions along a natural resource's commodity chain, one can establish the dynamics of control and maintenance of access to the economic benefits. Consistent with multiple reforms that have happened in Uganda notable among which are; decentralization, liberalization, and community-based natural resources management over the years, ACODE undertook research to elucidate the obvious increase in local participation and benefit sharing in the fishery sector. A key reform in the fishery sector in Uganda was the inception of BMUs and anticipation had been that this would lead to distributional equity of fishing benefits to communities. In CCAs, there is a special focus on the market, price, quantities and performance. There is also analysis of relations of power sources, uses of power and effects of exercise of power in a socially differentiated environment. The focus is also on political institutions and how they affect the existence and functioning of markets, with attention given to different market agents engaging in competitive as well as collective or collusive actions. It also looks at the regulatory environment.

Fisheries on Lake George

The NWP analytical framework is applied to the case study of Lake George fisheries to address the connection between poverty and the fisheries activities. The context of the fishery is described followed by the social groups and stakeholders involved. Lake George in Uganda is shared between the districts of Kasese, Kamwenge and Bushenyi. There are six official landing sites on the lake, with another two on the Kazinga Channel. The lake basin supports a population of about 13,000 people (UBOS, 2006), most of whom, live within the Queen Elizabeth Protected Area, parts of the Queen Elizabeth National Park and the Kyambura Game Reserve. Lake George is renowned both for its high productivity and its flagship bird species such as the Shoebill *Balaeniceps rex*. Over the years, the lake has attracted a lot of international attention. It was part of the International Biological Programme in the late 1960s. Becoming Uganda's first Ramsar site was a further recognition of the importance of the lake as a centre for biological diversity.

Located in Western Uganda, Lake George lies in the western branch of the Great East African Rift Valley. It is a small shallow lake with a mean depth of 2.5m and maximum of about 4m. It has a water surface area of 260 km^2 with a catchment area of 9,700 Km^2. The lake lies astride the equator at an altitude of 914m above sea level. The lake lies between 0:05 - 0:05S, and 30:02 - 30:18E. Numerous rivers, most of which originate from the Ruwenzori Mountains, feed Lake George. Some of the major river inflows include Rumi, Mubuku and Nsonge from Rwenzori and Mpanga and Dura from the northeast. The outflow is the Kazinga Channel, which drains toward Lake Edward. The northern lakeshore is lined with extensive permanent swamps of up to 21 Km long and 14 Km wide that occupy more than half the area designated as a Ramsar Site under the Ramsar Convention's List of Wetlands of International Importance in 1988. Most of the in-coming rivers pass through these permanent swamps. The lake has a single outlet, the Kazinga Channel, which drains to the southwest and runs for 36 Km into Lake Edward, another lake shared between Uganda and the Democratic Republic of Congo (Musinguzi *et al.*, 2003).

In hydrological terms, Lake George is remarkably stable. Despite its very shallow depth, seasonal changes in water levels are less than 1 metre, with highest levels occurring in May-June and November-January, shortly after the two seasonal peaks of rainfall. Water fluctuation levels are very low. About 75 per cent of the lakeshore is within the boundaries of the Queen Elizabeth Protected Area (QEPA), under the management of the Uganda Wildlife Authority (UWA). This has implications for use of the lake and for the livelihood strategies of people living at the fish landing sites' boundaries. The Rwenzori Mountains are an imposing feature of the basin, influencing the local climate and flow of water to the lake. The lake supports commercial fisheries, whose fleet size has been controlled by central Government through licensing since the 1950s.

Figure 6.2: Sketch Map of Lake George

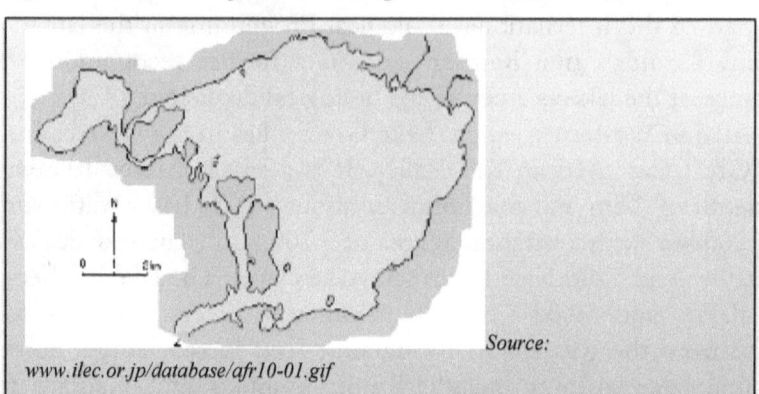

Source: www.ilec.or.jp/database/afr10-01.gif

Lake George is a rich environment supporting a highly productive fishery. Lake George is a habitat for a variety of fish species including, those considered to have been indigenous and now extinct in Lake Victoria. The main species caught and commercially exploited include Nile tilapia (*Oreochromis niloticus*) locally known as *Ngege*, *Protopterus aethiopicus* (*Emamba*), *Clarias gariepinus* (*Emale*) and *Bagrus docmak* (*Semutundu*). There are also other rare but occasionally caught species which include; *Oreochromis leucosti* (*Bambala*), *Barbus altianalis* (Enjunguli), *Mormyrus kannume* (*Kasulubani*) and the most quoted rare but valuable specie *Labeo forskalli/ victorianus* (*Eningu*). The fisher folk on Lake George indicate that the rate at which they were catching *Clarias* was increasing yet the specie is known to be among the most uncommon, an indication of a poor performance of the fishery (Balirwa *et al.*, 2003).

Lake George is naturally eutrophic resulting in an increased algae bloom, with a very high phytoplankton biomass which results in low water transparency. The lake maintains an extremely high rate of primary production throughout the year which is attributed to the rapid uptake of nutrients derived mainly from organic decomposition in the mud. The high rate of uptake is maintained by frequent, usually daily, disturbance of the bottom mud by winds due to the shallowness of the water. It is probable that the high rate of production has persisted with little seasonal variation since the origin of the lake in its present form and climatic regime are stable. The most remarkable feature of the lake compared with other tropical lakes is the high productivity coupled with the overall stability of the biomasses of its organisms. This, in turn, is due to the shallowness of the lake, its stable water level and the frequent winds in all seasons, which circulate nutrients from the mud more or less continuously (Musinguzi *et al.*, 2003).

Lake George presents potential fishery resources abundance but it is under stress due to the extra fishing pressure. All indications point at the resource being over exploited since too many people are chasing a few fish. This explains the notion that such a common natural resource cannot be responded to by the market controls alone. According to local knowledge, catching of hard-to-catch and self-preserving *Emale* for example is on the increase which indicates that nearly all *Tilapia* often caught with nets is getting finished.

Communities around the lake appreciate the fact that it is a divine natural resource and is for everyone, and that Government holds it trust of the people. They further believe that the lake belonged to their forefathers who managed it well. However, they are worried and concerned by the worsening rate at which the productivity of the lake is being affected. Open to imperfections in use of command and control and traditional approaches in managing a common property resource, a resource like a lake is vulnerable to overexploitation with dangers of possible collapse. It cannot survive if left to the forces of the market alone. It is necessary to have interventions that balance demands of human capital, growth factors of the resource (fish) and the desire to have sustainable use.

Lake George directly or indirectly supports a population of about 81,264 people. It is a major source of direct livelihood for most people. Paradoxically, a substantial segment of people in communities that depend on the lake fall in the category of the 'poor' yet the lake is a great source of wealth. Data available from Uganda Bureau of Statistics (UBOS) indicates that 39.6 per cent of people in Mahyoro sub-county – Kamwenge district, 46.5 per cent in Muhokya and Lake Katwe sub-counties in Kasese district and 58.2 per cent in Katunguru Bushenyi district are considered poor people.

In research for findings reported in this chapter, information was collected from local communities and perspectives from documents on the reasons for the decline in fish catch from Lake George. Several reasons emerged. The introduction of crocodiles into the lake by Uganda Wildlife Authority (UWA) was largely believed to have been a major cause of the decrease. General decrease in amount of rainfall was also known to be responsible for the reduced food for fish. Evidence of the receding lake size was seen in the expansion of the shoreline. The net result of reducing water levels was that fish ended up with nowhere to breed from, thus greatly reducing fish catches. Fishing pressure as a result of increased population around the lake could also explain a reduction in fish catches. Voices from the communities show recognition of the fact that the lake was a static resource yet the population dependant on it kept growing at a high rate.

> Kashaka landing site… used to support about 100 people, but now there are more than 500 people (personal communication).

Furthermore, poor fishing methods are known to account for reducing fish catches. Given the big family sizes, many fish consumers prefer to buy many smaller fish instead of buying one mature and big one. This is a push factor for fisher-folk opting to use small sized nets, to catch small-sized fish including immature ones because of their ready market. The increasing numbers of un-gazetted fish landing sites on the lake is known to have led to a reduction in fish catches. Community members neighbouring the lake are known to create their small, unmonitored and *'unofficial'* landing sites. Other factors contributing to reducing fish catches include; farming activities taking place on hill tops adjacent to the lake leading to silting during rainy seasons thereby destroying some of the fish breeding areas and reclamation of wetlands adjacent to the lake for rice growing.

The Main Actors in the Fishery Sector

A number of actors along the fish product chain act as conduits in whose hands wealth pass often leaving no visible impact. The actors can be classified into three categories, which are not mutually exclusive. The primary actors who extract fish from the lake include the *barias* and boat owners. The second group are those engaged in post-harvest handling of fish and include artisanal processors, *deyi-deyi* and traders. The last category includes local council administrators, overseers of resource extraction and handling (e.g. BMU officials) as well as organisations like Lake George Basin Integrated Management Organization (LAGBIMO). Understanding the relationship between the various actors and the fish resource, the nature of wealth distribution and the distribution of power and decision making authority are essential pre-conditions for establishing a management regime that responds to fish over-exploitation degradation and poverty reduction in fishing communities.

Fishermen *(Barias)*

In Uganda, fishermen are locally and commonly known as *"barias"*. This group is constituted exclusively by individuals of mostly male gender that move on fishing boats for the actual fishing activity. They constitute a majority of active people in a fishing community. Many of them claim to have been born and grown up in fishing villages while others report that they ended up in the business as ordinary job seekers from far off places. On average, there are 2-3 *barias* per fishing boat. Not all *barias* in a fishing village have access to a fishing boat every day. By virtue of their work, replete with risks (such as drowning, piracy, attacks by wild animals, extreme weather conditions etc), *barias* spend their daily incomes lavishly. The tendency to indulge in sex and alcohol is high. Their lack of frugality is based on their false belief that the lake has infinite resources. As a result, they are the most poverty stricken. However, *barias* vote and can be voted to be part of the BMU committees. According to the BMU Statute, *barias* constitute 30 per cent of the BMU committee.

Boat Owners

Boat owners are men and women who invest their money in the fishing business. They purchase fishing boats, boat engines, fishing nets and other equipment required to support fishing activity. They bear the risk of any kind in the invested capital and meet almost all the operating costs in the fishing business. They employ *barias* as fishing crew. Some boat owners are former leaders of landing site committees. In some cases, boat owners are former *barias*, while others still act as *barias* on their own boats. According to the BMU statute, the representation of boat owners on the BMU Committee in Uganda is 30 per cent. Owning a boat is a business that provides for at least a substantial daily income, unless there are no catches at all on a particular day. Once *barias* bring the fish catch, boat owners normally take 50 per cent of it and leave the remaining 50 per cent to be shared between the two or three *barias*. However, this sharing arrangement differs from one landing site to another.

Fish Mongers

These are individuals who buy fish as soon as it is delivered at the landing site and sell it to different markets benefiting from the difference in prices. Depending on the location of the markets, fish mongers commute from site to another buying fish and selling to different markets. Their role, as a service, is to make fish available to consumers. This category of actors wields power especially because of their ability to mediate between the demand and supply dimensions of fish which, makes this category relatively wealthy.

Artisanal Processors

This is a category of mainly women involved in small-scale fish processing by sun drying, smoking or salting and selling to fish mongers. Their role is mainly to add value and benefit from the price differences between raw and processed fish. In some cases, such processors act as fish mongers/traders as well. In most cases majority of artisanal processors fry *'Mugongo wazi'* (industrial fish rejects) which is a big shift in their (traditional) processing technology.

Transporters

This is a category of business people (virtually all men) who provide auxiliary service to fish traders. They offer transport services to the fish trade business and like other actors, their business depends on the volumes of fish traded. Transporters in the context of Lake George are low-scale pick-up truck owners, motorcycles or bicycles. On Lake Victoria however, and specifically for Nile perch trade, transporters double as fish mongers. They buy from the fishermen and sell to fish processing plants and benefit from the difference in prices. Often, they are able to dictate fish prices at the landing sites, as fish has limited shelf-life. As a result of this, the transporters are in position to dictate price differences between landing sites and at the final destination. Besides, it is noteworthy that the final fish prices are also a function of the prevailing fuel prices.

The 'Deyi-Deyi'

The '*deyi-deyi*' is a category of individuals (mostly young men and women) at landing sites who provide auxiliary services during the fishing landing and selling business. They neither participate in active fishing nor trading, but they live and survive on doing petty jobs and providing ancillary services such as selling tea and food to fishermen and other landing site communities. They provide other services such as off-loading fish from boats, cleaning and drying of nets. They at times buy fish from the boat and re-sell it making a tiny profit. Most members of this category are the indigenous people of the area, and their employment depends on the seasonality of the lake. If the harvest is good, they are able to earn more from the services they render. This is not a dominant group in the fish chain and is not captured in the chain analysis. Within the fish product chain, this is the group with the least power and who gain least from the fishing activity due to their informality. They can be members of the BMU assembly but their position is not represented on the BMU committee.

Beach Management Units (BMUs)

BMUs are community-based management organisations, legally set up at landing sites instituted to provide a co-management role of the fisheries resource ('The Fishing (Beach Management) Rules', 2003). Notable actors that constitute these organisations are boat owners, fishing crew, fish mongers and other fish stakeholders at respective landing sites. All members at a fish-landing site make up a BMU assembly, which elects a BMU committee to spearhead the core management of BMU activities. The representation of members on BMU committee is stipulated in the BMU Statutory instrument No. 35/2003 as 30 per cent boat owners, 30 per cent fishing crew, 10 per cent fishmongers and 30 per cent other stakeholder groups (listed in the BMU Statutory Instrument, including fish processors, boat makers, local gear makers or repairers, fishing equipment dealers, managers, and chatterers). For gender purposes, it is stipulated that women should constitute at least 30 per cent of the BMU committee. According to the regulations, a BMU executive has, *inter alia*, powers to recommend fishers for boat licences and fishing permits, collect revenue, enforce fishing rules and regulations, discipline its errant members (e.g. illegal fishers or those using illegal/destructive fish gear). BMUs are legally empowered to prosecute all persons flouting fishing rules and regulations and/or failing to do/satisfy any of the above requirements.

The Local Councils (LCs)

The Local Council (LCs) is the lowest level of local administration unit in the community, which are linked structurally to the village, parish, sub-county, districts and the central government. The LCs administers services on behalf of government. Their chairpersons are democratically elected and they, in turn, appoint deserving men and women on their executive committees. Their services often supplement BMUs services such as support to fisheries enforcement by Local Defence Units – an arm of the LC structure. However, on some landing sites, power conflicts are reported between LCs and BMUs, owing to a blurred demarcation line separating the powers of the LCI from a BMU at the local community level

Fisheries, Livelihoods and Well-Being

Quite clearly, fishing as demonstrated in the case of Lake George is a socio-economic activity that supports many people. Even when fishing is a survival resource of immense proportion, many categories of people that depend on it perceive themselves to be the poorest of the poor. An important question to interrogate is whether in reality, most fish-dependent communities are in actual fact poor or comparatively poor. It is also worthwhile to disentangle and elucidate social-economic dynamics that inform poverty perceptions in fishing populations. A substantial proportion of Ugandans depends on fish and fishing for livelihood and survival. The Ugandan National Environmental Management Authority (NEMA) estimates that fish makes up between 30-50 per cent of Ugandan's dietary protein and the fisheries sector employs 1.2 million people (Robinson, 2015). What is not in doubt is attempting to exactly map out the exact number of people whose livelihood solely depends on fishing. In the same vein, there is no precise information regarding the number of people whose livelihoods depend on Lake George fishery sector. Nevertheless, there is no doubt that a substantial proportion of the population around Lake George basin derive livelihood from fishing. The biggest group of people employed around the lake work as *barias*, and *'deyi-deyi'*.Boat owners are few, considering the investment capital needed to start the business.

The forms of employment for the different actors in the fish production and marketing can be categorised as, formal, informal, seasonal or permanent. Being a boat owner for instance is formal and permanent employment. Regardless of the reduced catches, the boat owner earns some money if his or her boat gone to the water. The *barias* have seasonal employment and the opportunity to be employed on a boat depends on one's relationship with the boat owner. The *deyi-deyi's* kind of work is both informal and seasonal, and varies according to the prevailing circumstances on the lake. Fish traders are permanently employed but their level of involvement largely depends on the catches.

The fishing sector is generally male-dominated as revealed in FGDs, involvement of women in the fishing sector is a recent phenomenon:

> In the past, women were not so much engaged in the fishing business. They concentrated more on making crafts from which they earned a living. It was after the realization that there was a lot of pressure being exerted on the swamp that the community decided to stop crafts making. Women then started to engage in fishing (personal communication)

> **Voices from the field**
>
> "...bye-laws are passed by the district, but people there don't know fishing...if such bye-laws are to be passed, one of us should go to explain what we need...you find like the chairman doesn't know nets..." **(An FGD at Mahyoro fish landing site – can you add dates to all the FGD viewpoints e.g. 28/10/2016).**
>
> "our colleagues farming in the hills...when they dig, soil runs into the lake...in road construction, the soil is washed into the lake...accumulating to about 10 meters...this affects breeding ground for fish..." **(An FGD at Kayinja fish landing site).**
>
> "...if given free nets .we would make sure that no one uses the wrong fish nets...in this lake, fish used to die due to its high density but not any more now...this is due to an increased population of people chasing it around..." **(An FGD at Katunguru Kasese fish landing site)**

No women work as *barias:*

> We think that women are not supposed to go into such dangerous water –they are a bit weak yet this is a very strenuous and physical job

(A Baria, personal communication).

> Most women at landing sites are *deyi-deyi* and participate in providing auxiliary services.

They are involved in fish trade both at landing sites and in markets, mending fishing nets, setting fishing nets (withstrengthened thread), preparing and selling meals (food, porridge, tea etc), selling and serving alcohol, and sometimes smoking and salting fish. Some women specialize in buying and selling *'by-catch'* and some are sex workers.

Other than fishing villages being generally overpopulated, inhabitants tend to be poor, lacking some basics like proper sanitation and performing poorly on all quality of life indicators. Discussions with *barias* and boat owners indicated that poverty in fishing communities is worsened by the decline in fish catches. It is not uncommon to be told that fisher folk defecate and urinate in the lake or by the lake banks.

For instance, fieldwork to collect data for this chapter found that fishing communities had no access to safe water. The main source of water supply was the lake itself. Such water was used for bathing, washing clothes, cooking and in many cases, fishermen drunk it unboiled. Could poverty be an inherent characteristic of fishing communities? Poverty has many dimensions and has been defined in many ways. Multi-dimensionally, poverty is not only a function of income level but also has health, nutritional and educational ramifications. Insecurity and social exclusion are also dimensions of poverty according to Poverty Eradication Action Plan (PEAP) findings. Fishing communities are generally characterised by poverty indicators which include poor housing structures, lack of basic health and sanitary facilities, poor road network, low education levels, among others. On Lake George, the fisher folk's lives are further characterized by landlessness. In communities around the lake, a rich person is described as one with at least two or three boats, and such individuals are difficult to come-by.

> . . . the daily income of a Baria may approximately be Ug. Shs.15, 000/= (about 4.1 US Dollars) which they spend in a day, mostly on alcohol and prostitutes. . . Most Barias at this site never bother to educate their children

The poverty problem at fish landing sites is further exacerbated by the tendency of each fisher to trade in their fish as an individual. Often times, this leads to exploitation, since many cannot effectively negotiate good deals. There are many middlemen in the fish product and marketing chain whose pay is embedded thereby reducing on the would-be income of the *barias*. Some of the middlemen could be done away with if the *barias* formed organised negotiating groups.

Many people in fishing communities do not save. They believe that there is constant income from the lake, and it is unnecessary to save. The culture of saving is not helped by the distances that an individual who wishes to deposit money in the bank has to travel to financial institutions. These communities would better be served by beach banks. Most *barias* are forever in debts because they get a lot of advance payments from many boat owners which they have to repay after going fishing. The *barias'* argument is that even when indisposed or weak, hence unable to go to the lake; they still need basic necessities like food and medicine. Therefore, they beg boat owners for advance payments in such situations with the hope of paying when they go out to the lake where they always hope to make a good catch. Secondly, *barias* report that they do not fear taking advance payments because they are used to getting a daily income and are sure that when they go to the lake, they will be able to get some catch. The reality is that a good catch is not a daily guarantee.

Attempts at having savings schemes to ensure some form of financial safeguard are undermined by the mobile lifestyle of most fishermen. One of the savings schemes that had been created on a landing site was found to have gone moribund because fishermen would be given money after which they would disappear with it. This discouraged many from entrusting people with their money. Others *barias* argued that they do not make savings because proceeds from the lake are very low and are mostly spent on daily up keep.

As seen from the case of Lake George, fishing has other associated non-monetary benefits. As a food, fish is an important and cheap source of animal protein. The overexploitation of this food source and the loss of employment are likely to affect people's nutrition. Fishing is a source of employment for large sections of the population living in the lake regions. The downside to unemployment is that the poorer fisher-folk become, the more they unsustainably exploit the fishery. Since time immemorial, the fisher folk living adjacent to lakes have always considered these lakes as a cultural heritage. The lake becomes not only a source of livelihood but a symbol of identity rooted in traditional cosmology. An influx of 'outsiders' to traditional fishing communities is common. Traditional fishing communities accuse the 'outsiders' of being responsible for the introduction of illegal fishing methods, believed to be destructive to the local aquatic environmental cultural heritage.

In the context of all the foregoing, it is safe to say that there are winners and losers in the fish-product chain. Though it is a poverty curse for some actors, fishing is an economic blessing for other actors. There is definitely a wealth axis in the fish productionchain. For instance, in spite of declining fish stocks in most lakes of a type like George, fisheries remain a venture with potential to generate wealth. Exploitation of existing fish stocks in value terms still constitutes a factor in poverty reduction among fish-dependent communities. Many wealth maps attempts to answer the fundamental question of why fishing communities remain poor (Development Assistance Committee, 2001) in spite of the natural wealth as translated into landed values of fish catch. In fact, fishing communities are the main channels of wealth and should therefore demonstrate characteristics of this wealth. Each fish sold passes through the hands of a fisherman and a boat owner leaving different levels of revenue.

The value of fish landed ashore is the assumed wealth of the resource in a given period. Although the added value of other multiplier effects are computed as part of the total wealth, research for this chapter assumed the value of annual fish landings as the natural wealth of the fisheries resources of Lake George in a given year. The analysis is extended to look at the extent to which this wealth is shared amongst a section of actors and how the sharing is reflected in the poverty levels of these actors in the Lake George fishery.

Table 6.1: Estimated Landed Value of Fish from Lake George 1950-2005

Year	Metric tones	Est. price Ushs/Kg	Est. Value Ushs '000	Est. Value USD Equivalent
1950-54	2,850	100	285,000	160,022
1955-59	2,800	150	420,000	235,823
1960-64	4,550	100	455,000	255,474
1965-69	3,850	350	1,347,500	756,597
1970-74	3,500	420	1,470,000	825,379
1975-79	3,950	500	1,975,000	1,098,821
1980-84	1,950	700	1,365,000	766,423
1985-89	2,200	1,000	2,200,000	1,235,261
1997	6,850	1,000	6,850,000	3,846,154
2000	3,200	1,200	3,840,000	2,156,092
2001 est.	3,500	1,100	3,850,000	2,169,707
2004 est.	3,580	1,300	4,654,000	2,613,139
2005 est.	3,650	1,500	5,475,000	3,074,116

Adapted from Kamanyi and Beyanga (1991) and projected to 2005.

Figure 6.3: Trends in Catches of Fish from Lake George (1950s – 2000)

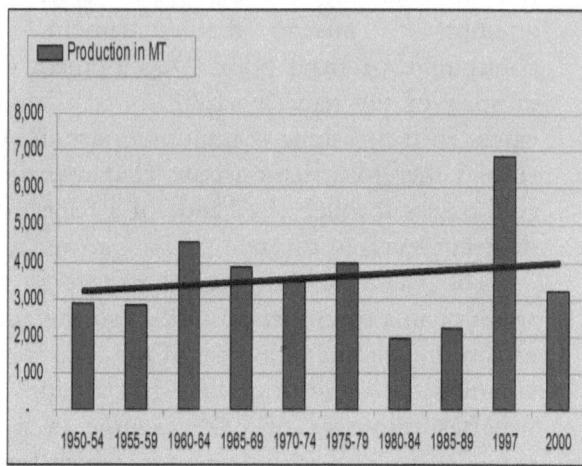

From the estimated figures, it can be seen from Table 6.1 and Figure 6.3 that the total wealth of Lake George in 2005, at the time of data collection was in the region of Ushs 4-5 billion annually (2-3Million USD). Any improvement in the collection of catch statistics certainly canshow that this value is even much higher.

In spite of this actual and potential wealth, the socio-economic status within fishery-dependent communities reflects a different reality. The main conduits of this wealth, especially fishermen and boat owners, are strikingly poor basing on the national poverty standards. Although there have been no disaggregated quantitative data on the poverty status of fishing communities, qualitative poverty assessment studies indicate that poverty is prevalent amongst fishing communities (MoFPED, 2002).

How then is fish-related wealth reflected in the poverty status of fish dependent communities as seen at Lake George? The analysis of wealth among some actors shows that some gains accrue to different groups in the fish product chain. There is also an indication of a mismatch between gains received and quality of life. To some actors like the *Barias* and fishmongers, the gains are not translated into poverty reduction or livelihood improvement.

Table 6.2: Gains and Margins Accruing to a Fisherman/Baria

Operating costs – variable:	Ushs per Day	Ushs per month	Ushs per Year	% of costs	%ge of landed value	Best case scenario
User fees (paid to tenderers)	500	15,000	180,000	11.1%	2.0%	500
Fuel & oil for fishing boats	-	-	-	-	-	

Payment to barias labour (wages)	1,000	30,000	360,000	22.2%	4.0%	1,000
Sub-total variable costs	1,500	45,000	540,000	33.2%	6.0%	1,500
Operating Costs – fixed		-				-
Baria's permit	14	420	5,040	0.3%	0.1%	14
Loan pay-back	3,000	90,000	1,080,000	66.5%	12.0%	3,000
Sub-Total fixed	3,014	90,420	1,085,040	66.8%	12.1%	3,014
Capital costs		-	-			-
Sub-Total Capital	-	-	-		0%	-
Total Costs	4,514	135,420	1,625,040	100%	18%	4,514
Revenue from total Sales:	25,000	750,000	9,000,000		100%	70,005
25% share of the baria	5,875	176,250	2,115,000			17,126
Profit (loss)	2,861	85,830	1,029,960			14,112
Profit (loss) as %ge of landed value	11.4%	11.4%				20.2%

Note that at the time this data was collected, the mean exchange rate of 1 USD to Uganda Shillings was 1,781 (Bank of Uganda, 2005)

Source: Developed by the authors from fieldwork data

The analysis in Table 2 shows that the value of daily catches of fishermen on Lake George ranged between Ushs 0 – 140,000/= (about 79 USD) per day per fishing boat. At the time of fieldwork to collect data for this finding, there were periods when boats landed with no catches and sometimes with high catches. In the worst case scenario, the value of catches would stabilize at Ushs 25,000 (about 15 USD) per day. As indicated before, the sharing arrangement of the landed value between the boat owner and *barias* differed from landing site to another. As already noted, every boat would have an average of two crew members. In most cases, boat owners and fishermen shared the landed value in the ratio of 2:1:1. With associated costs, the fisherman/*baria* would earn a net income of Ushs 2,861 per day, a figure that was slightly above the poverty line indicator of US$1 per person per day in Uganda.

In the best case scenario and which was always the case, the daily average value of catches approximated Ushs 70,000 (about 40 USD) per boat. Using the same sharing arrangement Ushs 70,000 would earn each *baria* Ushs 14,000 (about 7 USD) per day. Note that sharing is done after deducting the general costs such as payments of user fees to the tendered services, annual *baria's* permit and some payment as *baria's* wages. The computed daily, monthly and annual earnings for a *baria* is therefore net income. These earnings represent 11 per cent and 20.2 per cent of the landed value (or wealth of the resource) in the worst and best case scenario respectively. Using this analysis of earnings, the *barias* on the Lake George fishery are by no means poor. They only posses characteristics of poverty and this explains the common statements that fishing communities are among the poor in the country.

Following the above analysis and considering the *barias'* net daily income of Ushs 2,861, it represents an equivalent of Shs. 85,000 (about 48 USD) per month. This money was at the time of fieldwork for these findings higher than the salary of a Driver or Messenger working in a Government Civil Service job. Moreover, a government Driver or Messenger at the time who earned an average of Ushs 70,000 per month had to incur other costs of food and accommodation. A *baria* was better off than a Government Driver or a Messenger and yet Government Drivers were not considered among the poor, or at least did not possess poverty characteristics. The fishermen on Lake Victoria, on the other hand were much better off than fishermen on Lake George. This was because the value of a unit of fish from Lake Victoria was higher than a similar unit from Lake George. Past research had already computed the annual income of a *baria* from Lake Victoria to be about Ushs 3 million translated into a monthly income of 250,000 (about 140 USD) per month (Ikwaput-Nyeko, 2004).

Table 6.3: Gains and Margins Accruing to a Boat Owner

Operating costs - variable:	Ushs per day	Ushs per month	Ushs per Year	% of costs	%ge of landed value	Best case scenario
User/tender fees	500	15,000	180,000	16%	2.0%	500
Fuel & oil for fishing boats	-	-	-	-	-	-
Labour on nets	200	6,000	72,000	6%	0.8%	200
Sub-total variable costs	700	21,000	252,000	22%		700

Operating Costs - fixed						-
Repair & maintenance boats	200	6,000	72,000	6%	0.8%	200
Threads for tying nets	333	10,000	120,000	11%	1.3%	333
Labour for tying 30 nets	1389	41,667	500,000	44%	5.6%	1,389
Boat license	58	1,750	21,000	2%	0.2%	58
Income tax	61	1,833	22,000	2%	0.2%	61
Sub-Total fixed	2,042	61,250	735,000	65%		2,042
Capital costs		-	-			-
Boat	417	12,500	150,000	13%	1.7%	417
50 nets of 4.5" (@ 5,000)	695	20,850	250,200	22%	2.8%	695
Sub-Total Capital	1,112	33,350	400,200			1,112
Total Costs	3,153	94,600	1,135,200			3,153
Revenue from total Sales:	25,000	750,000	9,000,000		100.0%	70,000
50% share of the Boat owner	12,150	364,500	4,374,000			34,650
Profit (loss)	6,955	208,650	2,503,800			29,455
Profit (loss) as %ge of landed value	28%	28%	28%			42%

Note that at the time this data was collected, the mean exchange rate of 1 USD to Uganda Shillings was 1,781

Source: Developed by the authors from fieldwork data

The analysis on earnings among actors in the Lake George Fishery at the time of fieldwork for this chapter was extended to the boat owners under similar conditions used in the analysis of *barias*. In the fishing business, the boat owner's main investment capital was on nets and boat. Boats owners also incurred costs associated with depreciation of capital (boats and nets). Other costs included the operating capital of repair and maintenance of boats and payment of government taxes. Fishermen on Lake George did not use engines and therefore did not incur costs on fuel. The others costs incurred included payment of user fees which also constituted other forms of operating costs. In the worst case scenario and deducting total costs from the 50 per cent share of the landed value, the boat owner earned a net daily income of Ushs 6,955 (about 4 USD) which translated into a net monthly income of Ushs 208,650 (about 117 USD) and net annual income of Ushs 2.5 million (about 1,404 USD) representing approximately 28 per cent of the landed value – the assumed wealth of the resource in that year. This income was equivalent to an average salary of Primary School Teacher at that time. Using this figure, the boat owners were by no means wealthier than *barias* whose income was only 11.4 per cent of the landed value. In the best case scenario, where an average daily landed value went as high as Ushs 70,000; the boat owners daily income went as high as Ushs 29,455 representing a monthly income of Ushs 883,650 annual income representing 42 per cent of the landed value higher than the *barias* of 20.2 per cent. This income was higher than that of a Government Civil Servant in scale of U3 at that time. The earnings of the boat owner reflected the invested capital and therefore fishing to them was a business and not a means of survival.

Table 6.4: Gains and Margins Accruing to a Fish Monger

Operating costs – variable:	Ushs per Day	Ushs per month	Ushs per Year	% of costs
Raw material fish [10kgs of fish]	10,000	300,000	3,600,000	77%
Sub-total variable costs	10,000	300,000	3,600,000	77%
Operating Costs – fixed				
Transport from L/site to Market	3,000	90,000	1,080,000	23%
Local taxes - landing site				
license fees (fish movement permit)	28	833	10,000	0.2%
medical form (by health inspector)	4	125	1,500	0.0%
beach license	28	833	10,000	0.2%

Local taxes – market				
market dues	500	15,000	180,000	4%
other costs/stall hire etc	1,000	30,000	360,000	8%
Sub-Total fixed	3,060	91,792	1,101,500	23%
Capital costs				
Sub-Total Capital	-	-	-	
Total Costs	13,060	391,792	4,701,500	100%
Revenue from total Sales:	15,000	450,000	5,400,000	
Profit (loss)	1,940	58,208	698,500	15%
Profit (loss) as %ge landed value	8%	8%	8%	

Source: Developed by the authors from fieldwork data

The fishmongers on the other hand earned relatively lower than the *baria* and boat owner. The net profits of the fishmonger were in the region of 8 per cent of the landed value compared to 11.4 per cent and 28 per cent for *barias* and boat owner respectively. But their income was on average almost, if not less than the poverty index of US$1 per person per day. Table 5 summarises the annual margins amongst the three actors in the fish production chain. It can be deduced from their earnings that none of these is expected to reflect any signs of poverty based on their daily, monthly and annual earnings.

Table 6.5: Annual Earnings & Margins of Selected Actors in the Lake George Fish Chain (worst case scenario)

	Boat owner		Baria		Fish monger	
Earnings	Daily	Annual	Daily	Annual	Daily	Annual
Total earnings ('000 Ushs)	12.1	4,374	5.9	2,115	15	5,400
Margins/Profit (Loss)['000 Ushs]	6.9	2,504	2.9	1,030	2	699
Profit (loss) as %ge of landed value		28%		11%		8%

Source: Developed by the authors from fieldwork data

The boat owners, followed by the *barias*, were a wealthier category of individuals on the landing sites based actors on Lake George fish chain as represented by distribution of net income and as a percentage of net assumed wealth. In spite of these levels of wealth, some boat owners possessed characteristics of poor people. At the same time, they owned land and properties in their village locales. They paid school fees for their children and were able to even invest in buying more boats.

In summary, the *Barias* remained poor in spite of the wealth associated with fish. Characteristically, they have different perceptions as to why they remain poor. Many *Barias* consider a lake to be an infinite resource with inexhaustible fish stocks. Consequently, they extravagantly spend what they derive from a day's catch with the confidence that another day on the lake will pretty much enable them earn similar or a better living. It also true that being on the lake is replete with a lot of risks. Whenever they land ashore, *barias* psychologically feel that they have been given *'a new lease of life in the world'*. In a celebratory mood after a triumphant return, they indulge in alcohol and having fun with prostitutes, thereby ending up with no saving. Benefits from the landed fish catch are shared between the *barias* and boat owner and the sharing formula is not uniform across fish landing sites or lakes.

Conclusion

In spite of the negative perceptions about most fisher folk being poor, they continue to live and ache out a living from the fish resource. Their survival off the lake as the case is on Lake George is that the BMU rules give power to BMUs over ownership and management of the fishery at each fish landing site. BMUs have powers to enforce rules and apprehend wrong-doers in the fishing business. These BMUs act on behalf of the Chief Fisheries Officer. Their capacity to enforce rules is however limited by inadequate financial resources. Institutionally, fisheries management in Uganda is vested in the Department of Fisheries Resources (DFR) under the Fisheries Act. At the district level, DFR links with the District Fisheries Office under the office of the Chief Administrative Officer to manage fisheries resources. At community level, fisheries management is undertaken by the Beach Management Units.

In many situations, BMUs work with Local Councils to ensure proper management of the lake. People desirous of starting fishing activities on the lake in such situations make their intentions known to the first level of a Local Council (village or ward) and then, to the BMUs. In some fish landing sites, BMUs were working well with the Local Councils. At times, there were tensions within BMUs around Lake George. For instance, some BMUs refused to remit the 25 per cent accruing from sales of the fish movement permits. The failure to remit such monies frustrated and undermined the development of any fisher infrastructure on the landing sites.

Information obtained indicated that there was substantial revenue remitted to the relevant Local Governments form fisheries. This remitted revenue included; taxes and charges such as user charges in form of tender fees, market dues, boat licenses and fisherman's permit. Past analysis indicates that these fees amount to 2 per cent of the value of landings. Not only were the communities expecting to receive services in return for the taxes they pay, but also Local Government regulations require that a proportion (25 per cent) of the collected revenue be remitted back to the lowest Local Council. However, the reality in a number of visited communities reveal that power wielding official at the LC-III and local governments hardly remit the 25 per cent to the lowest level and in a few cases, did not disclose the amounts. Moreover, there are public infrastructures, such as sanitation facilities, fish handling slabs etc. built for the use of communities by Local government who collect these fees.

Power, as wielded by boat owners and *barias*, influences resource management, ownership and distribution of gains. Power in this case is a function of each individual's inputs into the business. The boat owner, being the owner of the fishing gear and thus the employer of the *baria*, commands more influence and benefits from the business. It is important to note that the advent of BMUs reduced the powers of the boat owners; and being the owners of the capital, they wield sufficient power as demonstrated by their ability to hire and fire the *barias*.

The ascendancy of BMUs to positions of power eclipsed the traditional fishing leaders, the *Gabungas*, most of whom were boat owners and these were the custodians of fisheries activities. Therefore, some respondents were of the view that traditional leaders wield a wealth of knowledge about the management of the lake since they had stayed and lived on the lake longer than any other category. The sharing of revenue from the catch is more often than not based on mutual agreement between boat owners and *barias*. This sharing arrangement is often uniform on a particular landing site but varies in other landing sites. In spite of this formal sharing arrangement, some *barias* who tend not to declare all the catch but sell it to on the lake fish traders and/or unofficial landing sites. This unfair advantage to the boat owners helps the *barias* to get more income though still is not translated into a change in their wealth status. With skewed power relations between the different participating categories in resource distribution, there was bound to emerge inequities in fisheries income distributions.

Being owners of capital, boat owners are inclined to conservation and engagement in legal and acceptable fishing methods. Similarly, *barias* argue that they too adhere to conservation efforts since they own nothing and have less likelihood of wrong-doing in the form of using wrong-sized fishing nets. However, both actors are not innocent when it comes to matters of depleting the lake of fish. Both reinforce one another's undisciplined fishing methods in other to out-do competitors. Besides, the 'open access' property regime prevailing on the lake is far from being an optimum environment to mitigate against destructive fishing.

Fishing communities are aware and appreciate that the fishing policy that advocates for use of at least a $4^1/_2$ inch fishing nets. Discussions with different actor reveal that some of the BMUs and District Fisheries Officers are weak which brings to light the need to have a stronger body to enforce fishing regulations if the lake fish are to be rejuvenated. Some actors worry about delays in acquisition of fishing licences and permits. This perpetuates unregulated fishing.

Co-management entails the integration and application of both scientific and traditional knowledge to conserve and manage fisheries resources, by allowing the devolution of much of the decision-making and data collection to the communities living in the area (Farlinger, 1997).Fisheries co-management forms part of integrated lake management and empirical evidence demonstrates that centralized approaches to fisheries management have not prevented fish stocks from declining and livelihoods being threatened. To this end, fisheries co-management approaches have been proposed extensively in Uganda to improve fisheries governance, resource productivity and livelihoods.

Initially, fishing communities were not involved in fisheries management or setting rules and regulations nor were there any efforts to harness and build on the knowledge and experiences of the local fisher folk. Secondly, communities were not powerful enough to demand for quality services that could help reduce their income poverty. Since the Beach Management Unit legislation is in place, there is a massive opportunity to reduce poverty amongst these resource-dependent communities by adopting a management model that puts fisher folk at per with other stakeholders including Government. With active involvement of fisheries communities in management of the resources upon which their livelihoods depend, it is expected that illegal and harmful fishing practices will be reduced; resource productivity will increase resulting in higher fish catch and incomes.

In light of the evidence from this case study, we conclude that the fishery enterprise is an important resource with potential for wealth creation. However, the socio-economic status within fishery-dependent communities on the lake reflects a different reality. The main conduits of this wealth, especially *Barias* and *deyi-deyi*, are characteristically poor. *Barias* who are the biggest group of actors on Lake George in particular and all fishing communities in general have work routines that are replete with risks such as drowning, piracy, attacks by wild animals, extreme weather conditions etc. As a consequence, perhaps, they spend their daily incomes lavishly, on sex workers and alcohol. Their inability to save and invest part of their daily incomes is backed by a false belief that the lake has infinite resources. It is such wasteful lifestyles that render such actors to appear as characteristically poor. While the underplaying hypothesis was that investments to increase the economic value of natural resources (in this case fish) *per se* might not lead to poverty eradication and environmental sustainability, findings suggest that other factors need attention as well. We argue that the overemphasis on resource conservation without corresponding emphasis on the power, economic relations and behavioural patterns among the actors largely account for the perceived marginal successes in interventions aimed at ameliorating poverty among fishing communities. Future research could elucidate more on the influence of power on the behavioural aspects of living in a fish-landing site.

References

Balirwa, J. S., Chapman, C. A., Chapman, L. J., Cowx, I. G., Geheb, K., Kaufman, L., R.H. Lowe-McConnell, O., Seehausen, Wanink, J. H., Welcomme, R. L. and Witte, F. (2003) 'Biodiversity and fisheries sustainability in the Lake Victoria basin: an unexpected marriage?', *Bioscience*, 53, pp. 703–716.

Bank of Uganda (2005) 'Foreign Exchange Rate (Uganda Shillings per USD)'.

Development Assistance Committee, O. (2001) *The DAC Guidelines: Poverty Reduction*. Paris: OECD.

FAO (2000) *A Handbook for defining the setting up a food security information and early warning system (FSIEWS)*. Food and Agriculture Organisation of the United Nations Rome.

Farlinger, S. (1997) 'Selected Issues in Fisheries Management', in Gallaugher, P., Vodden, K., and Wood, L. (eds) *Exploring Cooperative Management in Fisheries*. Vancouver, BC.: Pacific Fisheries Think Tank.

'Fish (Beach Management) Rules' (2003).

Ikwaput-Nyeko, J. (2004) 'Co-management and value chains: the role of the Nile perch exports in poverty eradication in Lake Victoria fishing communities'. Reykjavik, Iceland: United Nations University Fisheries Training Programme.

Kamanyi, J. R. and Beyanga, P. M. (1991) 'The fishery resources of Lake Edward (Uganda portion), mode of exploitation and management', in Ssentongo, G. (ed.) *Compilation of the papers presented at the technical consultation on Lakes Edward and Mobutu*. Kampala: UNDP/FAO Regional Project for Inland Fisheries Planning (IFIP), p. 86.

Keizire, B. B. (2003) 'Relevancy of Fisheries in Uganda's Economy', *A document to support the revision of the Poverty Eradication Action Plan (PEAP)*.

Maaif (2011) 'Department of Fisheries Resources Annual Report 2010/2011'. Available at: http://aquaticcommons.org/20470/1/Dfr Annual Report 2012.pdf.

Mofped (2002) *Second Participatory Poverty Assessment Report: Deepening the Understanding of Poverty*.

Musinguzi, K. A., Nunan, F. and Scullion, J. (2003) 'Integrated Management of Lake George, Uganda. The Lake George Basin Integrated

Management Organisation (LAGBIMO)', *Paper presented at a regional Workshop on Lake Management Initiatives in Africa.* Nairobi Kenya.

Nema (2004) *State of Environment Report by National Environment Management Authority.*

Raikes, P., Jensen, M. F. and Ponte, S. (2000) 'Global Commodity Chain Analysis and the French Filiere Approach: Comparison and Critique', *Economy and Society*, 29(3), pp. 390–417. doi: 10.1080/03085140050084589.

Robinson, J. (2015) 'Fisheries resource management and peace-building in Uganda and DRC', *A New Climate For Peace Blog.* Available at: https://library.ecc-platform.org/news/fisheries-resource-management-and-peacebuilding-uganda-and-drc.

Tanzarn, N. and Bishop-Sambrook, C. (2003) *The dynamics of HIV/Aids in small-scale fishing communities in Uganda.* FAO Rome: GTZ.

'The Fishing (Beach Management) Rules' (2003) *Statutory Instrument*, 35.

The Poverty Eradication Action Plan (PEAP) (2004). Available at: http://www.uac.go.ug/policies.htm#peap.

Ubos (2006) *2002 Uganda Population and Housing Census: Analytical Report.* Kampala. Available at: https://www.google.com/url?sa=t&rct=j&q=&esrc=s&source=web&cd=1&cad=rja&uact=8&ved=2ahukewjjon6nl77gahuqbwmbhxq6b Aqfjaaegqiabac&url=https%3A%2F%2Fwww.ubos.org%2Fonlinefiles%2Fuploads%2Fubos%2Fpdf%2520documents%2F2002%2520Census PopnSizeGrowthAnalyticalReport.pdf&usg=AOvVaw0uoGqRzIM1QB BGOwmHs-us.

USAID and Africa Bureau (AFR/SD) (2002) *Nature, wealth, and power: emerging best practice for revitalizing rural Africa.* Washington, DC, USA: USAID in collaboration with CIFOR, Winrock International, WRI, IRG. Available at: http://pdf.usaid.gov/pdf_docs/Pnacr288.pdf.

CHAPTER SEVEN

Management of National Oil Companies: Lessons for Uganda

Dan Ngabirano

Introduction

Emerging oil producing countries such as Uganda must decide on how best to manage the process of developing their newly found resource in order to realize maximum benefits for their citizens and contribute to sustainable livelihoods. The state must decide on whether to solely shoulder the entire responsibility or to share this responsibility with private actors. The decision for the most part depends on the prevailing social, political and economic circumstances in the country. Historically, a number of emerging oil producing countries, especially those outside Europe and the USA, have relied on International Oil Companies (IOCs) for exploration and development of their petroleum resources. This is explained by a number of factors, but perhaps the most compelling of these being that emerging oil producing countries often lack the relevant technical expertise and funds to invest in a very risky yet capital intensive and challenging sector. For these same limitations, some developed countries in Europe and the USA opted to entrust the exploration and development of their petroleum resources to Private Oil Companies (POCs) rather than the state. The tendency to entrust exploration, development and other related oil activities to IOCs and POCs is increasingly being reversed and resource rich states are slowly reclaiming this role by forming their own National Oil Companies (NOCs). These are state owned companies that are created to exercise direct control over the country's petroleum resources on behalf of the state. NOCs are increasingly becoming powerful actors in global trade to the extent that they control over 90 per cent of the world's oil reserves and 75 per cent of all oil production (Tordo *et al.*, 2011). Well governed National Oil companies are increasingly becoming relevant in ensuring that development of oil and gas resources contribute to sustainable wealth for its citizens.

The Uganda National Oil Company (Natoil) is established under the Petroleum (Exploration, Development and Production) Act of 2013 hereinafter referred to as the Upstream law ('Petroleum (Exploration, Development and Production)', 2013a). Under this law, Natoil is to be wholly owned by the state and is responsible for managing the country's commercial interests in all petroleum activities. Although it is not yet very clear how much stake government will have in oil activities, early indications show that the government of Uganda will have a 17 per cent - 18 per cent stake in all oil production and up to 40 per cent in the refinery (*Tullow: National Oil Company may share in production, but government must make up its mind over basin development, Oil in Uganda,* 2012; *A Good Deal Better? Uganda's Secret Oil Secrets Explained, Global Witness,* 2014; Ojambo, 2013). It will be the responsibility of Natoil to manage these stakes on behalf of government.

The National Oil Company is expected to play a very significant role in the development of the country's petroleum resources currently estimated at 6.5 billion barrels (Directorate of Petroleum, Ministry of Energy Minerals, 2014). However, this will only be possible if the company is properly governed and managed in accordance with recognized standards and good practices. The purpose of this charter is to look at a number of these standards and practices and from this suggest lessons for best management of the Uganda National Oil Company (Natoil). This chapter is structured into four parts; Part 1 is the introduction to the study, Part 2 deals with the history and evolution of NOCs, Part 3 provides an overview of Natoil taking into consideration lessons and experiences from Norway and Nigeria. Part 4 contains conclusions to the study.

History and Evolution of National oil Companies

The history and evolution of NOCs is important in understanding some of the considerations behind the formation of NOCs as well as the diversities that exist in majority of the NOCs around the world. The history is also helpful in the determination of whether indeed NOCs around the world have been successful in fulfilling the purpose for which they were established. This is critical to emerging oil producing countries like Uganda who have chosen to establish NOCs to perform specific tasks.

State Intervention and NOCs

The evolution of NOCs has been described as a cyclical experience constituting of three major phases: a) direct state intervention; b) liberalization/privatization; and c) reversion to state intervention. The first phase constituting of direct state intervention in the petroleum industry has been traced back to the efforts of the Austria Hungary Empire to deal with an excess in the resource production prompted in 1908 (Heller, 1980). In response to a production outburst, Emperor Franz Joseph ordered for construction of a state topping plant to utilize and add value to the excess crude oil produced. This marked the entry of the state into an industry that had for long been dominated by Private Oil Companies (POC). The Austria-Hungary experience was followed by a number of other European countries. In the case of Britain and France, NOCs were created to ensure a steady supply of the much-needed oil during World War I (World Bank, 2018). The limitations of the private sector and the rising importance of oil as a strategic resource were therefore responsible for the initial formulation of NOCs especially in Europe. In the face of a weak private sector, states became the best alternative investor in oil activities considered unattractive to the private sector yet important for national security.

Outside Europe, NOCs were next established in Latin America where significant amounts of oil reserves had been discovered in the 1920s after ousting Spanish backed colonialists. Argentina was the first to establish a NOC in Latin America by founding Yacimientos Petroliferos Fiscales (YPF) in 1922. Several other Latin American countries including Chile, Uruguay, Peru, Mexico and Bolivia followed suit with each establishing its own NOC. In all these countries NOCs were formed to protect and manage state interests in the newly discovered resources.

In the Middle East, the formation of NOCs was greatly inspired by the rise in the demand and prices for oil after World War II. This greatly improved the negotiation capacity of oil rich countries in the region that had until that moment had to rely on the expertise and financial muscle of IOCs. The power of these oil rich countries was further bolstered by the formation of the Organization of Oil Producing and Exporting Countries (OPEC) in 1960 ('OPEC Brief History', no date). As a block, the organization amplified the voice of its individual member countries in the face of powerful and often intimidating IOCs. For instance, at its initial meeting in 1968, OPEC issued a Declaration of Policy for its member countries. The Declaration emphasized sovereignty over the resource by host nations and made a strong recommendation for direct state participation in resource management ('OPEC Brief History', no date).

OPEC efforts to promote state intervention were sealed by the Arab-Israel war of 1973 which resulted into placement of an oil embargo on the west and its domineering IOCs. The embargo nationalized all aspects of the resource and shut out IOCs. This cemented state control over the oil resource in the Middle East and NOCs were formed to exercise this control on behalf of the state. In response to OPECs growing influence and the embargo, a number of western states also formed special NOCs to regulate domestic production and explore ways of recovering the lost production. One of the NOCs formed to counter OPEC influence was the British National Oil Company (BNOC) (Vickers and Yarrow, 1988).

In Africa, the formation of NOCs was majorly inspired by the grant of self-rule following the end of World War II. As a symbol of this newly found independence, some oilproducing countries established NOCs to manage the resource on behalf of the state. The aura of independence was boosted by the UN Declaration of Permanent Sovereignty over Natural Resources, which among others, emphasized the right of States to resources found on their territories ('Declaration of Permanent Sovereignty over Natural Resources 1962-GA Resolution 1803 XVII', 1962). Consequently Algeria was the first African country to establish a NOC in 1965, followed by Libya in 1970. In sub-Saharan Africa, Nigeria became the first country to establish a NOC in 1971. This was followed by Angola in 1976 and eventually Chad in 2006.

Table 7.1: Select NOCs and Year of Formation
Source: World Bank 2011.

Country	NOC	Year
Argentina	YPF	1922
France	CFP	1924
Italy	Agip	1926
Mexico	Pemex	1938
Saudi Arabia	Petromin	1962
Algeria	Sonatrach	1965
Iraq	INOC	1967
Libya	LNOC	1970
Nigeria	NNPC	1971
Norway	Statoil	1972
Malaysia	Petronas	1974
Angola	Sonangol	1976
Equatorial Guinea	GE Petrol	2002
Chad	SHT	2006
Uganda	Natoil	2013

Liberalization and Privatization

By the end of the 1970's most NOCs had not performed to expectations and this forced a number of governments, especially those in the western world, to sell their stake in these companies to the private sector(Stevens, 2004). In most of the cases, governments maintained a minority stake while entrusting the majority stake with private companies (Stevens, 2004). During this time, the concept of state ownership and intervention collapsed and a general belief that governments had no business in the market place emerged (Stevens, 2004). This belief was validated by the inefficiencies with which most SOEs operated and the debt crisis experienced in the 1980's which made it even more difficult for states to sustain a great number of these enterprises. In the circumstances, a great majority of SOEs resorted to borrowing from the World Bank and the IMF (Stevens, 2008).

In the Middle East and Latin America, NOCs were equally affected by the fall in oil prices experienced in the 1980's. The drop in prices meant that these countries, especially those in Latin America could not depend on oil alone and in this vulnerable state, they succumbed to World Bank and IMF pressures to adopt stabilization programs (Tordo, 2007). Argentina led the way by privatizing its major oil companies and opening up the highly state monopolized oil sector to competition (Tordo, 2007). The Argentina experience which succeeded in the shortest run was adopted by a number of other oil producing countries.

The other factor that contributed to the decline of state intervention and reduced the prominence of NOCs was the fall of the Soviet Union. This marked the effective fall of socialism, an idea that had influenced the formation of NOCs in some parts of the world. In the newly created states such as Kazakhstan and Azerbaijan for instance, the collapse of socialism as an ideology drove NOCs to the periphery and opened up opportunities for IOCs and POCs.

Privatization of NOCs was further accelerated by the general feeling that NOCs had become too powerful to the extent of threatening state power. This created a situation of a state within a state where the NOC is not accountable to state structures. The fact that most NOCs operated with very minimal budgetary support from their governments also made them more independent (Hartshorn, 1993). Lastly, for their budgetary limitations a number of NOCs failed to attract sufficient technical expertise (Al-Mazeedi, 1992). For this reason, countries had no option but to turn to IOCs especially where complex geology was involved. IOCs were better equipped in terms of expertise and resources and had the ability to undertake risky ventures unlike NOCs.

Return to State Intervention and Re-Birth of NOCs

As observed at the beginning of this section, the evolution of NOCs was a cyclic process rotating between the reliance on the private sector for development of petroleum resources and direct state involvement in resource development.

Following a long spate of privatization and liberalization of the petroleum sector in the 1980's and 90's largely as a result of the decline in oil prices and subsequent imposition of stabilization programs on net oil producing and net oil importing countries by the world Bank and IMF, many countries took a turn back to direct state involvement in the early 2000's.

Privatization and liberalization of oil only delivered short term gains and failed to deliver in the long term, forcing countries to resume direct intervention. This time however majority countries assumed a measured role by taking over what they considered strategic and leaving the rest to the private sector. In effect, in the 2000's, governments and the private sector enjoyed a shared stake notwithstanding that in many cases the governments often had the more dominant say.

In addition to the failure of privatization and liberalization to deliver as expected, the rebound in world oil prices greatly contributed to the rebirth of NOCs in many parts of the world (Stevens, 2008). In 2005 the price of oil shot from USD 12.21 a barrel in 1998 to USD 54.5 (Stevens, 2008). Further more by November 2007, the price had moved up to over USD 100 for a barrel of oil. The recovery of oil prices coupled with the failure of privatization and liberalization therefore led countries to reconsider the idea of state intervention in petroleum resource activities. It is for this same reason and the reality of petroleum as a resource of strategic importance that a number of emerging oil producing countries have insisted on forming NOCs to protect their national interests, while at the same time allowing for a measured role of the private sector.

Table 7.2: Current Trends of NOC Ownership in Select Countries

NOC	% of state ownership
CNOOC Ltd- China	66%
ENI- Italy	30.30%
ONGC-	84.23%
Pemex	100%
Petrobas	55.7%
Petronas	100%
Statoil- Norway	67%
Sonatrach- Algeria	100%
NNPC-Nigeria	100%
Sonangol- Angola	100%
GE-Petrol- Equatorial Guinea	100%
SHT- Chad	100%
Natoil- Uganda	100%

Source: World Bank (2011).

Reasons for the Formation of NOCs

Historically, NOCs were formed to counter the influence of IOCs most especially in Africa and the Middle East (Hartshorn, 1993). The whole idea that IOCs were foreign was contested in countries that had recently gained independence (Hartshorn, 1993). In these countries, IOCs represented a continuation of imperialism. Against this background, it was important for these countries to form NOCs as a symbol of independence and an alternative to foreign companies. The establishment of NOCs also represented the restoration of a sense of national pride and an end to foreign domination.

Related to the above, a number of countries constituted NOCs to champion national interests. Unlike IOCs whose biggest motivation is to increase shareholder value, NOCs were believed to promote a broad range of national interests (MacPherson, 2003). In countries where they were formed NOCs were expected to, among other things, create jobs and develop the capacity of locals; support the development of infrastructure as well as the provision of key social services such as health and education. In effect NOCs would deliver beyond the purely commercial purpose, by supporting government programs even if these were not necessarily related to their activities.The importance of

Reasons for Creation of NOCs	
1.	Counter the influence of IOCs/ State sovereignty over natural resources;
2.	Promote national interests & benefit from associated linkage's such as industrial & infrastructural developments employment &delivery of basic services ;
3.	Source of financing political and economic programs
4.	Vehicles for control of strategic resources like oil ; and
5.	Rent maximization through reduction of information asymm-tries.

petroleum as a strategic resource is yet another reason for the creation of NOCs.

Petroleum since its discovery has been a key driver of many economies around the world. The supply and production of this important resource has therefore for long been considered too important to be left to the market hence the need for government intevention (Ro binson,1993). NOCs became the most appropriate vehicles for realizatio n of state control over this strategic resour-ce (Robinson, 1993).

In some places NOCs were established to enable governments to benefit from political gains that flow from state control of petroleum as a strategic resource. Government control over petroleum resources enhances the bargaining power of the state and enables the state to use its wealth to secure funding for its political, military and economic programs. Direct control also ensures that the state is in position to influence a number of decisions necessary for generating local support such as employment and pricing of petroleum products (Cheon et al., 2015).

Additionally, NOCs were favored for being excellent vehicles for rent maximization (Tordo, 2007). Since a number of emerging oil producing countries lacked the administrative and fiscal machinery to extract rents from petroleum, formation of the NOC was believed to provide for direct state role of the state in the collection of rents.

Moreover, NOCs were considered more effective in monitoring the activities of private oil companies. The direct involvement of the NOC in oil activities ensured that governments obtained first-hand information and experience of what takes place in the sector to guide their own operations (Grayson, 1981).This way government would be able to effectively monitor the sector and maximize returns in the long run. Finally, in some cases NOCs were formed solely to serve ideological purposes. At the peak of socialism some countries such as Algeria viewed the creation of state oil companies as the most appropriate way to implement the socialist agenda (Madelin, 1974).

Ugandan National Oil Companies and International Best Practices

Uganda follows the Regulatory Best Practice (RBP) in the management of its petroleum resources. (*Uganda National Oil Policy, Principle 7.2*). This is akin to the highly acclaimed Norwegian model of petroleum governance that seeks to separate the commercial role from other roles such as regulation. The Petroleum (Exploration, Development and Production) Act therefore entrusts the management of the country's resources in three main institutions ('Petroleum (Exploration, Development and Production)', 2013a). These include the Directorate of Petroleum in the Ministry responsible for oil and gas (*Uganda National Oil Policy, Principle 7.2*). The Petroleum Authority ('Petroleum (Exploration, Development and Production)', 2013b), and the Uganda National Oil Company ('Petroleum (Exploration, Development and Production)', 2013b). Each of these three institutions is assigned a specific role and under the law Natoil is responsible for the management of all the commercial aspects of the resource ('Petroleum (Exploration, Development and Production)', 2013b).

Establishment and Roles

Natoil is established under the Petroleum (Exploration, Development and Production) Act hereinafter referred to as the Upstream Act ('Petroleum (Exploration, Development and Production)', 2013b). Under the law, the national oil company exists as a body corporate whose role is to manage Uganda's commercial aspects of petroleum and the participating interests of the state in petroleum agreements. The other functions of Natoil under the law include among others; marketing the country's share of petroleum received in kind; managing business aspects of state participation; developing expertise in the industry; optimizing shareholder value; participation in joint ventures on behalf of the state; and the responsibility to propose petroleum activities that the government should be involved in locally and internationally. The role of Natoil is therefore restricted to serving the commercial purpose under the law. This is progressive and accords to recommended practice.

There are a number of potential dangers where the NOC is entrusted with significant non-commercial functions such as regulation, job creation, advancement of local capacity, infrastructural development, income redistribution and state borrowing among other things. First there is a risk of conflict of interest if the NOC is to exercise a non-commercial function as regulation alongside its commercial role. Secondly most of these non-commercial functions are capital intensive and present a real burden on the NOCs financial resources. For these reasons, it is recommended practice for NOCs to serve solely commercial purposes.

Ownership of Natoil and Governance of the Uganda NOC

The sole ownership of Natoil is placed in the hands of the state ('Petroleum (Exploration, Development and Production)', 2013b). As observed above, the law requires the Uganda NOC to be incorporated under the Companies Act 2012. The Companies Act recognizes two types of companies namely; private companies and public companies. A private company is one whose membership ranges from 1 to 100 members while a public company is one that is not a private company. The challenge with the upstream law is that it does not prescribe as to which of the two forms of companies Natoil should take. In the circumstances under the registered Articles and Memorandum of Association, Natoil was incorporated as a private company in 2015.

In terms of ownership, the Ministry of Energy owns 51 per cent and the remaining 49 per cent of the Company's shares is owned by the Ministry of Finance. This effectively vests in the government of Uganda 100 per cent ownership of the NOC. Experiences elsewhere demonstrate that there is a lot of value in having the NOC ownership shared between government and private actors. As observed above, for the NOC to be efficient, it should strictly serve a commercial role and should be in position to compete with the rest of the actors. As it is, private actors unlike governments often have an edge in terms of experience and business skills. A partnership between government and the private sector therefore brings a lot of value and greatly enhances the productivity of the NOC. In addition, the private sector is a source of cheap capital into which NOCs can tap to finance their activities.

For the above reasons a number of countries with NOCs prefer to divest part ownership in the NOC to the private sector. One approach to this has been to list the NOC on domestic and international stock exchanges. Norway is a good example of a country where this approach has succeeded. The Norwegian government owns 67 per cent of Statoil while the rest is vested with private actors. The recently enacted Nigerian Petroleum Industry Governance Bill also supports part-private investment in the country's NOC. Under this law which was passed in May 2017, there is a requirement to divest to the public up to 30 per cent of the shares in the state oil company with in a period of six years following the establishment of the NOC (Nigerian National Petroleum Corporation, 2018b).

It light of the benefits of private investment in the petroleum sector, the Ugandan government should seriously consider granting ownership stake to different groups of private investors following a clear and transparent process. This will further the main objective for which Natoil was set up i.e. promoting commercial interests of the state.

Governance matters if Natoil is to achieve the various objectives for which it was established. Governance here is considered at three levels namely; internal governance, external governance and public scrutiny/oversight. External governance concerns the interaction between the state and the NOC while internal governance is about the institutional arrangements put in place for effective functioning of the NOC. Internal governance relates to aspects of board composition and structure, board powers, human resource and decision making processes among others. Public scrutiny is about the ability of citizens to participate and influence NOC activities through increased openness and transparency.

It is common practice for resource dependent countries to exercise majority control over the state oil company. The main reason advanced for this approach is the need to maximize petroleum rent. Uganda is not any different and the state enjoys a lot of control over Natoil; being the sole owner of the NOC. Although Natoil is yet to be fully operationalized, aspects of state control are quite evident in the law that establishes the NOC. For instance, the Board of Directors is appointed by the President, and the Minister must be informed of every matter that the Board intends to submit to the annual general meeting (Nigerian National Petroleum Corporation, 2018b). Further, the Minister is entitled to issue directions to the NOC in respect to exercise of its management task.

These provisions entrench state control over Natoil and expose the NOC to the risk of political interference in its work. This is problematic as politicians are bound to use the NOC to achieve their own interests. Political interference also puts political expedience above other considerations. This in turn opens the NOC to corruption and patronage, all of which are political tools that have been used in a number of failed resource rich countries to maintain the government of the day in power. In the event it is suggested that the role of the state in Natoil should be reduced to enable the NOC function independently (Heller *et al.*, 2014).

In terms of internal management, the law establishes a Board of Directors under Section 44 (1). Board functions are contained in Section 44 (2) and include, among other things; the responsibility to make annual plans including those regarding projects of major significance to state participation. The Board is also required to report on budget features for the coming year and to develop an annual report and accounts in respect to participating interests of the state.

It is acknowledged that the idea of having a Board of Directors is a good one. The challenge, as pointed out above is that the board is appointed by the President with the approval of Parliament (Nigerian National Petroleum Corporation, 2018b). Aside from the political burdens on appointees, there is an issue as to the competence of board members since the law does not outline any specific qualifications for board members. Neither does the law expressly bar appointment to the board where there is a manifest conflict of interest. The President is therefore left with an overwhelming discretion in terms of whom he can appoint as board member, which altogether puts the process at the risk of yielding political appointees rather than technically skilled ones. This in turn affects board performance and ultimately the operations of Natoil.

Although the Articles and Memorandum of Association of Natoil contain a number of provisions on board qualifications and tenure that are not sufficient given Uganda's context. As already mentioned the government of Uganda is at the moment a sole shareholder in Natoil and in that respect can take decisions including those that touch on amendment of the Articles and Memorandum of Association. To guard against such a step, important provisions such as those to do with board qualifications and tenure should be entrenched in the upstream law since then the decision to alter any of the provisions will ultimately fall on Parliament and not the executive which is now famous for taking decisions based on political expediency.

Moreover, under the law the Board is required to report to the Annual General Meeting (AGM) on all matters of social and political significance as well as those with significant social economic effects ('Petroleum Industry Bill', 2012, Section 44 (3)). In addition to this, it is the responsibility of the board to submit audited accounts and an annual overview of the country's participating interests in the sector to the annual general meeting ('Petroleum Industry Bill', 2012, Section 45).

The requirement to report to the AGM is a good attempt at enhancing transparency and accountability in Natoil. The challenge is that the annual general meeting in this case is constituted of one share holder, that is, the government of Uganda. Provisions regarding reporting and accountability to the AGM can only be meaningful where there is more than one shareholder as has been emphasized above. In this respect, it is strongly argued that rather than report to the sole shareholder, the Board should report to the Parliament of Uganda since petroleum resources are held by the government in trust for Ugandans. In particular, the board should submit a copy of the NOCs financial statement and audited report to Parliament annually. This information should also be made public in accordance with internationally acknowledged standards such as the Extractive Industries Transparency Initiative (EITI).

Beyond the requirement of the Board to submit annual audited accounts, it is not clear on whether accounts are subject to both internal and external audits. It is important that the accounts of the NOC are subjected to both audits. This not only strengthens accountability but also boosts the confidence of the true shareholders i.e. the citizens of Uganda in the NOC.

Still on the Board, the law is silent on the work of separate committees ordinarily constituted to complement the work of the board. These include the audit committee, compensation committee, safety and ethics committee and the nomination committee. The role of the audit committee is to ensure that the NOC complies with audit, accounting and financial standards. The compensation committee determines the terms and conditions of employment for the Chief Executive Officer of the NOC and other members of top management. The safety, sustainability and ethics committee ensures that the NOC is compliant with the NOCs safety, security, and sustainability and ethics policies except those that are related to finances.

Over and above, the upstream law as it stands does not incorporate a corporate governance framework under which Natoil should be governed. Similarly the Companies Act 2012 makes it optional for private companies such as Natoil to adopt a code of corporate governance. Only public companies are mandated by law to incorporate a code of corporate governance under the law .("The Companies Act, 2012', 2012).

Corporate governance generally refers to procedures and processes according to which an organization is directed and controlled (OECD, 2005a). It involves an attempt to find the balance between commercial and social roles while at the same time balancing individual interests with those of the community ('Report of the Committee on Financial Aspects of Corporate Governance', 1992). In the context of state owned companies such as Natoil, corporate governance entails the following features; effective board functioning, equal treatment of shareholders, business ethics, transparency and accountability(OECD, 2005b).These are extremely important for any SOE like Natoil to succeed and it is regrettable that in the case of Natoil, these principles are not mandatory (Kyepa, 2012).

Table 7.3 Summary of NatOil's Strengths and Weakness

Strengths	Weakness
Natoil focus on commercial activities Vis a Vis non-commercial purposes such as regulation and provision of basic services.	Appointment of the Board by the President as opposed to a nomination committee is subject to abuse and puts the NOC at a risk of political patronage.
Approval of appointed board members by Parliament	Absence of board committees such as the audit, corporate, ethics and compensation committees.
Board requirement to report to the AGM annually.	Manifest disregard of a corporate governance framework under which the NOC should operate.
Internal audit requirement	No provision for a mandatory external audit.
No special privileges for NOC creating competitiveness in the sector.	Sole ownership of NOC by state which creates a risk of political interference and denies NOC access to cheap capital for carrying out its operations.
	No clear provisions on funding of the NOC. The funding provided in the form of share capital (UGX 10billion) is not adequate to facilitate NOC activities especially in the early stages.

Source: Developed by the author

Experience of Select NOCs and Lessons for Uganda

NOCs have the potential to play a central role in the transformation of a country's petroleum resources. This, however, depends on how well they are managed. Poor NOC management breeds inefficiency and creates opportunities for corruption. Unfortunately, this has been the experience in many African countries; a number of which have sizeable amounts of oil reserves with very big potential.

Natoil is responsible for Uganda's commercial interests in the newly found petroleum resources and will play a huge role in ensuring that citizens benefit from this resource. For this reason it is important that right from the beginning, the company is properly managed and governed. This section highlights experiences of NOC management from two leading petroleum producing countries, that is, Norway and Nigeria. Of these, Norway is credited for being highly successful while Nigeria on the other hand has not been very successful in utilizing its NOC to secure maximum benefits for its citizens.

The Norwegian Oil Company (Statoil) and its Experiences

Norway is the largest oil producer in Europe and tenth in the world. As of 2008, the country's proven reserves were estimated at 7.5 billion barrels (Norwegian Petroleum Directorate, 2009). In addition to oil, Norway is also known for its huge natural gas reserves which were estimated at 78.2 trillion cubic feet as of 2008. As of today, Norway is the fifth largest producer of natural gas in the world.

Norway stands out among countries which have successfully used their petroleum wealth to transform their economies and the lives of their citizens. The country's success is attributable to its excellent management system over its resources right from the beginning. The Norwegian model of management also known as the 'trinity' involves the interaction of three separate agencies namely the Ministry of Petroleum and Energy (MPE), the State Oil Company (Statoil) and the Norwegian Petroleum Directorate (NPD). Under this model, there is a clear separation of responsibilities and each of the three entities is charged with a different role. (Tordo *et al.*, 2011). Furthermore, the MPE is responsible for formulation of policy, the NPD is responsible for regulation of the sector while the National Oil Company (Statoil) is charged with corporate strategy.

In playing a strictly commercial role, Statoil has made a significant contribution to the success of the petroleum industry in Norway in which it controls 80 per cent of the total oil production (Tordo et al., 2011). By 2011, statoil owned the biggest refinery in Norway i.e. the Mongstad refinery. At about the same time Statoil was reported to own stakes in two foreign refineries, one in the Netherlands (10 per cent) and the other in Denmark (100 per cent) (Tordo et al., 2011). In addition to this, the company enjoyed joint ownership of a petro-chemical plant in Denmark and operated in a total of 20 countries outside Norway.

Establishment and Roles

The Norwegian Oil Company was established in 1972 to pursue the state's commercial interests in the petroleum resources and to maximize the value and potential of the Norwegian Continental Shelf (NCS) while at the same time profitably increasing international production. To achieve these objectives, Statoil was granted some special privileges at the start of its activities (Tordo et al., 2011). In particular, Statoil was allowed a minimum participation of 50 per cent in all exploration activities and had the option to scale this up to a total of 80 per cent upon the confirmation of commercial deposits. This said, it should also be noted that from the beginning, Norway avoided the trap of having its NOC monopolize activities in the petroleum sector. As part of this strategy, Statoil's special privileges were revoked to among others stem its influence on national politics in the 1980s (Tordo et al., 2011).

The other factor that had the effect of the taming the monopoly of Statoil was Norway's admission into the European Economic Area in 1994 (Tordo et al., 2011). Under this arrangement, member countries were required to award licenses over their NCS competitively and any kind of discrimination in favor of state companies was prohibited. This opened up the NCS to a number of POCs with which Statoil had to compete. This created an opportunity for Statoil to benchmark its activities with those of other private companies greatly improving its competitiveness. With a history and experience of competitiveness and high levels of efficiency, Statoil found it east to venture into several other countries outside Norway without any major difficulties. To date, Statoil operates in 36 countries around the world and operates just like any other IOC. Six of these are African countries, including Algeria, Libya, Angola, Mozambique, Tanzania and Nigeria (Tordo *et al.*, 2011).

Ownership and Governance of the Norwegian Oil company

At the time of its creation, Statoil was wholly owned by the state and this remained the case for a period of 35 years. The decision to privatize part of the company was first made in December 2000 when Parliament approved the listing of 19.2 per cent of the company's shares on the Oslo and New York stock exchanges. Further listing approvals were made in 2004 and 2005 bringing down the total state stake in Statoil to per cent

In 2007, Statoil was merged with Norsk Hydro another partially state-owned oil company to form a new company Statoil- Hydro. In this new company, the government of Norway owns 67 per cent of the shares and the remaining 33 per cent is owned by the state pension fund and other private owners. The government's stake in Statoil is managed by the Ministry of Petroleum and Energy (Norwegian Ministry of Trade, 2015). Despite the fact that the government is the majority shareholder in the NOC, Statoil enjoys strong independence in its operations. Most decisions are made by the established institutional structures in accordance with provisions of the law that governs public companies ('Norwegian Public Limited Liability Companies Act of 13 June 1997', 2014). State influence over the NOC, if any, is extremely limited and instead management decisions are vested in the main organs of the NOC which include the Annual General Meeting (AGM), Board of Directors (Board), Corporate Assembly, Nomination Committee and Board committee ('Procedure for the Corporate Assembly of Equinor ASA', 2013). It should also be pointed out that no public official sits on the Board of Statoil. The board is constituted by independent directors and employees' representatives.

In terms of internal governance, the AGM which is required to be held by the end of June every year is the company's supreme organ and is responsible for electing the board and selecting members of the Corporate and Nomination Committees (*Corporate governance*, 2019). The

AGM also appoints the external auditor and approves all financial reports.

The other important organ of the NOC is the Board of Directors whose main role is to monitor day to day management and business activities of Statoil (*Corporate governance*, 2019). The board also appoints the company's top executives who include the Chief Executive Officer (CEO) and President. The mandate and conditions of service of these top executives is also determined by the Board. In addition to this, the board deals with a wide range of other company matters which include; security and safety, sustainability, corporation strategy, business plans, annual returns, reporting, compensation, leadership assessment and ethical matters among others.

In the execution of its work, the Board is assisted by three committees, that is, audit committee, compensation and safety committee and the sustainability & ethics committee. The Audit Committee is entrusted with the responsibility of recommending to the board the choice of external auditor (*Corporate governance*, 2019). Its major role, however, is to ensure that the group has an effective internal and external auditing system. The safety, ethics and sustainability committee on the other hand assists in supervision of the Company's safety, security, sustainability and ethics policies. Finally, the Compensation and Executive Development Committee assists the board in setting the terms and conditions of employment for the CEO and other top executives.

In terms of structure, the board is comprised of a total of 11 members whose term of service is two (2) years. Of these, eight (8) are independent directors and the remaining three (3) are employee representatives. Independent directors are required to have long standing experience in the petroleum sector, corporate governance, finance and legal disciplines.

Moreover under the Public Companies Act of Norway, in addition to internal structures, every company with more than 200 employees is required to have a Corporate Assembly (CA) and Nomination Committee. The key roles of the CA are to elect members of the Board and to oversee the Board and CEO management of the company. It is also the duty of the Assembly to advice on investment decisions of a considerable magnitude. In the case of Statoil, the Corporate Assembly is constituted by 20 members of which twelve (12) are elected by shareholders and the remaining eight (8) are elected by the company's employees (*Corporate governance*, 2019).

The Nomination Committee on the other hand is constituted of three (3) independent directors elected by the AGM and a representative from the Ministry of Petroleum and Energy. It's major role is to recommend to the AGM persons eligible for appointment to the CA. The Committee also makes a recommendation to the CA in regard to election of members of the board of directors. It is also the role of the nomination committee to come up with proposals for remuneration of the Board and members of the CA (Corporate governance, 2019).

In addition to its well constituted organs, Statoil has a Code of good corporate governance. The code aims at promoting among other things shareholder equality, transparency, performance, value creation, board independence and good societal relations (Corporate governance, 2019).

Nigeria National Petroleum Company - NNPC

Oil in Nigeria was first discovered in 1956 but commercial production only commenced in 1958 (Nigerian National Petroleum Corporation, 2019). From an initial 5,100bpd the country's oil production levels grew to 2.4million bpd by 2005 making Nigeria the largest oil producer in Africa (The World Bank, 2019). Nigeria also has the biggest natural gas reserves in Africa and is among the top five liquefied natural gas exporting countries in the world (Energy Information Administration, 2017). The Nigerian economy is therefore by and large oil driven and petroleum accounts for more than 90 per cent of the country's gross earnings. At the end of 2015 alone, Nigeria is reported to have earned an estimated USD 41.8 billion from its petroleum exports (Organization of the Petroleum Exporting Countries, 2018). This notwithstanding, a significant number of Nigerians remain poor as it is estimated that over 60 per cent Nigerians live below the poverty line with very limited access to basic services such as health and education (BBC News, 2015).

The majority of Nigerians have clearly not benefited from the country's petroleum resources contrary to expectations of many at the time of discovery of the resource (Walker, 2009). Petroleum has turned into a curse rather than a blessing as a result of the high levels of corruption, nepotism and environmental degradation (Walker, 2009).

This has turned communities in areas where oil is produced against oil companies often sparking off violent conflict.

The failure of Nigeria to use its enormous petroleum resources to transform the country and turn around the lives of its citizens demonstrates the importance of good governance in the management of petroleum resources. As already mentioned above, the petroleum sector in Nigeria has for a long time been punctuated by corruption and general mismanagement of the resource by the very entities created to develop the sector. The state oil company which was created to champion the country's development of its oil wealth is one of those institutions that have contributed to this state of affairs.

Establishment, Role and Governance of NNPC

The Nigeria National Petroleum Corporation (NNPC) was established in 1977 ('Nigeria National Petroleum Corporation Act No. 33 of 1977, Cap 320', 1990). Right from the beginning, the main mandate of the NNPC was to engage in all commercial activities that relate to the petroleum industry while at the same time enforcing regulatory measures through its Petroleum Inspectorate department ('Nigeria National Petroleum Corporation Act No. 33 of 1977, Cap 320', 1990).

The law bestows on the NNPC a number of duties and responsibilities in the course of all petroleum development stages i.e. upstream, midstream and downstream petroleum stages ('Nigeria National Petroleum Corporation Act No. 33 of 1977, Cap 320', 1990, section one (1)). In particular, the NNPC is charged with such duties including; petroleum exploration and prospecting, oil refining and processing, petroleum marketing, pipeline operation and the construction of handling equipment among others. In fulfilment of these duties, the NNPC enjoys a number of powers and privileges. It may hold property and enter into contracts and partnerships with any other firm or company in furtherance of its mandate. The Corporation also has powers to establish and maintain subsidiaries for the purpose of discharging its duties. Pursuant to this provision, the NNPC was split into twelve (12) subsidiary companies in 1988.

In insisting that the NNPC plays both commercial and regulatory roles, the law contributed to its eventual failure to meet the purpose for which it was established. Experience from successful countries such as

Norway suggests that for a NOC to succeed it must be assigned a specific purpose (MacPherson, 2003). Non-commercial purposes unnecessarily overburden the NOC's resources and prevent it from focusing on its core mandate. Secondly, by participating in commercial ventures in the petroleum sector while at the same time exercising the regulatory function, there is a big risk of conflict of interest on the side of the NOC. This kills competition and prevents the NOC from performing optimally as resources are instead invested in providing services that should ordinarily be provided by governments. In the case of Nigeria, burdening the NNPC with non-commercial responsibilities has greatly contributed to the poor performance of the NOC and ultimately the petroleum industry which it was meant to develop.

The Nigerian government owns 100 per cent of the Nigeria National Petroleum Corporation (NNPC) (Nigerian National Petroleum Corporation, 2018a). State ownership in the NNPC is exercised by the Ministry of Petroleum resources. As the sole owner, the state exercises significant control over the NNPC. For instance the government appoints 4 of the 12 board members of the NNPC and the Minister of Petroleum is the chairman of the board ('Nigeria National Petroleum Corporation Act No. 33 of 1977, Cap 320', 1990, section one).

Sole ownership and direct state influence over the activities of the NOC is problematic. In the case of the NNPC, politicians have taken advantage of state ownership to further their own political interests in the process diverting the NNPC from serving the mandate for which it was established. This has entrenched political patronage and corruption and is responsible for the huge losses that the NNPC has suffered over the years. According to an audit undertaken by the World Bank in 2000, it was estimated that the NNPC loses over USD 800million every year to corruption (World Bank Group, 2000). This does not include monies spent in providing costly fuel subsidies estimated to be USD 7 billion (*The Economist*, 2011).

In terms of internal governance, the NNPC is run by a Board comprised of twelve directors ('Nigeria National Petroleum Corporation Act No. 33 of 1977, Cap 320', 1990; The World Bank Group, 2008). These include the Minister of Petroleum Resources who is also the board chair, the Managing Director, six executive directors and four government appointees. The role of the board is to set strategy, approve projects and all contracts concluded by the NNPC. The Board however has limited control over the corporation's budget since all revenues are remitted to the state. Its role is simply to prepare a draft budget that is subject to approval by the Parliamentary Committee of Petroleum Resources. The challenge is that in most cases the NNPC is only allocated part of the funds requested leaving a big budget deficit. In these circumstances, the NNPC has no other option but to resort to external borrowing in order to sustain its activities sometimes circumventing the law (Alohan *et al.*, 2013). In 2007 for example, out of an estimated budget of USD 15.2 billion, the NNPC was only allocated USD 4.9 billion. The remaining USD 3.8 billion was sourced from the NNPC's partners and commercial banks (Alohan *et al.*, 2013). Under these circumstances the NNPC has constantly failed to deliver on its mandate.

In 2012, President Goodluck Jonathan appointed three special task forces to investigate activities of the NNPC in a bid to improve transparency and accountability in the oil sector. The three include the Petroleum Revenue Special Task Force, the Governance and Control Task Force and the National Refineries Committee. Investigations of the Petroleum Revenue Special Task Force revealed that an estimated USD 29 Billion was lost to corruption and mismanagement over a period of ten years (*Nigeria: 'Oil-gas sector mismanagement costs billions'*, 2012). The task force also found that an additional USD 6Billion was lost to oil theft. On its part, the Special Task Force charged with establishing Corporate Governance and Controls in the NNPC recommended for the scrapping of the NNPC and in its place a NOC that is commercially focused and internationally competitive formed (Ribad, 2012). Further, the Special Task Force recommended that the newly formed NOC be privatized and shares sold to Nigerians and other institutional investors with the government owning only 49 per cent stake. According to the Special Task Force, this would help in capitalization of the NOC that has for long been starved of finances.

These recommendations found their way into the proposed Petroleum Industry law of 2012 which seeks to introduce the legal, fiscal and regulatory reforms in the Nigerian petroleum industry (Nigerian National Petroleum Corporation, 2018b). Review of the laws is important step on the long journey to correcting mistakes that have befallen the Nigerian petroleum industry. As Nigeria embarks on the long journey to correcting the mistakes made in management of its resources, countries like Uganda must learn from this experience and strengthen management of their own petroleum sectors if they are to transform the newly found oil wealth into shared prosperity of its people.

Conclusion

In 2013, the Natoil was established under the Upstream Petroleum law to manage the state's commercial interests in the petroleum resource. Although Natoil is yet to be fully operationalized, there is a lot of hope among Ugandans that it will deliver the much anticipated benefits from the country's newly found resource. This is not a far-fetched expectation since NOCs have the potential to play a significant role in the development of their country's petroleum wealth. Their success in this regard however depends on how well organized and governed these companies are. Good corporate governance requires that the NOC is run independently and in the interests of all stake holders be it shareholders or members of the general public. For this to happen, the NOC must operate in a transparent manner and should be accountable. This can be achieved by among others setting up of competent and independent boards, establishment of functional internal and external audit systems and setting up of separate board committees to deal with matters of appointments, ethics, strategy and compensation among others. The importance of being well governed is clearly demonstrated by the varied experience of Norway and Nigeria both of which decided to entrust ownership of their vast petroleum resources in state owned companies. Right from the beginning Norway invested in strong governance systems for its NOC i.e. Statoil by strengthening transparency and accountability systems while placing corporate governance at the fore front. On the other hand NNPC has been associated with corruption and poor performance. This is because unlike Statoil, the NNPC did not invest in strong governance controls. The varied experience of the two countries provides powerful lessons that Natoil must take into consideration if it is to succeed in delivering to the expectations of Ugandans. Currently, board members and top executives of Natoil are appointed by the President which exposes the NOC to patronage politics as has been the case with NNPC. In addition, there is no provision for independent board committees and a mandatory external audit. From the Norwegian experience, such structures promote accountability and improve on the efficiency and effectiveness of NOCs.

References

A Good Deal Better? Uganda's Secret Oil Secrets Explained, Global Witness (2014). Available at: https://www.globalwitness.org/reports/good-deal-better/.

Al-Mazeedi, W. (1992) 'Privatizing the national oil companies in the Gulf', *Energy Policy*.

Alohan, J., Awom, U. and Odemwingie, E. (2013) 'Nigeria: US 1.5 Billion Fuel Debt Loan by NNPC Illegal- NASS', *All Africa*.

BBC News (2015) 'The Number of Nigerians Living in Poverty Rise to Near 61%'.

Cheon, A., Lckner, M. and Urpelainen, J. (2015) 'Instruments of Political Control: National Oil Companies', *Oil Prices & Petroleum Subsidies*. CPS, 48(3).

Corporate governance (2019) *Equinor*. Available at: https://www.equinor.com/en/about-us/corporate-governance.html (Accessed: 15 February 2019).

'Declaration of Permanent Sovereignty over Natural Resources 1962-GA Resolution 1803 XVII' (1962). December.

Directorate of Petroleum Ministry of Energy Minerals (2014) *Uganda's Petroleum Resources Increase to 6.5 Billion Barrels Oil in Place*. Petroleum Department. Available at: http://www.petroleum.go.ug/news/17/Ugandas-petroleum-resources-increase-to-65-billion-barrels-oil-in-place.

Energy Information Administration (2017) *Total Petroleum and Other Liquids Production 2017*, *EIA Beta*. Available at: www.eia.gov/beta/international/?fips=NI (Accessed: 16 February 2019).

Grayson, L. E. (1981) *National Oil Companies. Chichester: Wiley*. UK: National Oil Companies:John Wiley, Chichester.

Hartshorn, J. E. (1993) 'Oil Trade: Politics and Prospects'. Cambridge: Cambridge University Press.

Heller, C. A. (1980) 'The Birth and Growth of the Public Sector and

State Enterprises in the Petroleum Industry', *State Petroleum Enterprises in Developing Countries*. New York: Pergamon Press/United Nations Centre for Natural Resources, Energy and Transport.

Heller, P. R. P., PaashaMahdavi and Schreuder, J. (2014) 'Reforming Nationals Oil Companies, Nine Recommendations, Natural Resource Governance Institute'.

Kyepa, T. (2012) 'Integrating the Proposed National Oil Company of Uganda Into the Corporate Governance Discourse, Lessons from Norway', *Journal of Energy & Natural Resources Law*, 30(1).

MacPherson, C. (2003) 'National Oil Companies: Evolution, Issues,Outlook', in Davis, J. M., Ossowski, R., and Fedilino, A. (eds) *Fiscal Policy Formulation and Implementation in Oil Producing Countries*. Washington D. C: IMF.

Madelin, H. (1974) *Oil and Politics*. London: Saxon House/Lexington Books.

Nigeria: 'Oil-gas sector mismanagement costs billions' (2012) BBC News. Available at: https://www.bbc.com/news/world-africa-20081268.

'Nigeria National Petroleum Corporation Act No. 33 of 1977, Cap 320' (1990) *Laws of the Federal Republic of Nigeria*. Available at: http://www.nigeria-law.org/Nigerian National Petroleum Corporation Act.htm.

Nigerian National Petroleum Corporation (2018a) *About NNPC*. Available at: http://www.nnpcgroup.com/AboutNNPC/CorporateInfo.aspx (Accessed: 16 February 2019).

Nigerian National Petroleum Corporation (2018b) *Petroleum Industry Bill*. Available at: http://www.nnpcgroup.com/petroleumindustrybill.aspx (Accessed: 15 February 2019).

Nigerian National Petroleum Corporation (2019) *History of the Nigerian Petroleum Industry*. Available at: NNPCBusiness/BusinessInformation/OilGasinNigeria/IndustryHistory.aspx (Accessed: 15 February 2019).

Norwegian Ministry of Trade, I. and F. (2015) *The state ownership report 2015*. Available at: https://www.equinor.com/content/dam/statoil/documents/the-state-ownership-report-2015.pdf.

Norwegian Petroleum Directorate (2009) 'Facts'. Available at: http://www.npd.no/Global/Engelsk/3 Publications/Facts/Facts2009/Chapters/Kap4.pdf.

'Norwegian Public Limited Liability Companies Act of 13 June 1997'

(2014). Available at: https://www.oslobors.no/ob_eng/obnewsletter/download/20fd77664bccdf3f6b8cb0dc95eeb7bb/file/file/Norwegian Public Limited Liability Companies Act.pdf.

OECD (2005a) *Cooperate Governance, Glossary of Statistical Terms*. Available at: https://stats.oecd.org/glossary/detail.asp?ID=6778 (Accessed: 24 January 2019).

OECD (2005b) *Guidelines on Corporate Governance of State Owned Enterprises*. Available at: http://www.oecd.org/corporate/ca/corporategovernanceofstate ownedenterprises/oecdguidelinesoncorporategovernanceofstate-ownedenterprises.htm.

Ojambo, F. (2013) 'Uganda Draws up Plan for National Oil Company to Steer Industry', *Bloomberg*. Available at: http://www.bloomberg.com/news/articles/2013-06-06/uganda-draws-up-plan-for-national-oil-company-to-steer-industry.

'OPEC Brief History' (no date). Available at: http://www.opec.org/opec_web/en/about_us/24.htm.

Organization of the Petroleum Exporting Countries (2018) *Nigeria, Facts and Figures*. Available at: https://www.opec.org/opec_web/en/about_us/167.htm (Accessed: 16 February 2019).

'Petroleum (Exploration, Development and Production)' (2013a). Available at: http://pau.go.ug/uploads/Petroleum_EDP_Act_2013.pdf%0A.

'Petroleum (Exploration, Development and Production)' (2013b) *Act No. 3*.

'Procedure for the Corporate Assembly of Equinor ASA' (2013). Equinor. Available at: https://www.equinor.com/content/dam/statoil/documents/corporate-governance/equinor-procedure-for-the-corporate-assembly-15-may-2018.pdf.

'Report of the Committee on Financial Aspects of Corporate Governance' (1992).

Ribad, M. N. (2012) 'As Task Forces Submit Reports, Oil and Gas Sector Reform enters another Level', *This Day Live*. Available at: http://www.thisdaylive.com/articles/as-task-forces-submit-reports-oil-gas-sector-reform-enters-next-level/129604.

Robinson, C. (1993) *Energy Policy: Errors, Illusions and Market Realities*. London: the Institute of Economic Affairs.

Stevens, P. (2004) 'National Oil Companies: Good or Bad? A Literature Survey', *CEPMLPInternet Journal*, 14(10). Available at: https://www.dundee.ac.uk.

Stevens, P. (2008) 'National Oil Companies and International Oil Companies in the Middle East: Under the Shadow of Government and the Resource Nationalism Cycle', *JELB*, 1(1).

'The Companies Act, 2012' (2012), (1), pp. 1–253. Available at: https://ulii.org/system/files/legislation/act/2012/1/companies_act_no_1_of_2012_pdf_84470.pdf.

The Economist (2011) 'Nigeria's Subsidies: End them at Once', December.

The World Bank (2019) *The World Bank is helping to fight poverty and improve living standards for the people of Nigeria with more than 130 IBRD loans and IDA credits since 1958*, Africa Can.

The World Bank Group (2008) *A Citizen's Guide to National Oil Companies: Part B - Data Directory*. Washington D.C.: The International Bank for Reconstruction and Development/The World Bank. Available at: siteresources.worldbank.org/INTOGMC/Resources/NOC_Guide_B_Data_Directory.pdf.

Tordo, S. (2007) *Fiscal Systems for Hydrocarbons: Design Issues*. Washington D. C: World Bank.

Tordo, S., Tracy, B. S. and Arfaa, N. (2011) 'National Oil Companies and Value Creation: Case studies', *World Bank Working Paper*. Washington D. C, (218).

Tullow: National Oil Company may share in production, but government must make up its mind over basin development, Oil in Uganda (2012). Available at: http://www.oilinuganda.org/features/infrastructure/tullow-national-oil-company-may-share-in-production-but-government-must-make-up-its-mind-over-albertine-basin-development.html.

Uganda National Oil Policy, Principle 7.2 (no date).

Vickers, C. and Yarrow, G. (1988) *Privatization: Economic Analysis MIT Press*. Massachusetts: Cambridge.

Walker, A. (2009) 'The Day Oil as Discovered in Nigeria'. BBC News. Available at: http://news.bbc.co.uk/2/hi/africa/7840310.stm.

World Bank (2018) *Working paper*.

World Bank Group (2000) *NNPC Management Audit*. (December).

CHAPTER EIGHT

Conclusion

Ronald Naluwairo and Onesmus Mugyenyi

There is ample evidence that good governance is important for sustainable natural resource management and sustainable livelihoods. This is particularly so for economies that are natural resource based like Uganda. The biggest question is whether African Governments are doing enough to promote good governance of their countries' natural resources, and if not, what still needs to be done. Focusing on forestry, fisheries and the extractive (oil and gas) sub-sectors, this book sought to examine selected resource governance issues and highlight the critical gaps that still need to be addressed.

Chapter 1 dealt with the conceptual aspects and the linkage between the two concepts of 'natural resource governance' and 'sustainable livelihoods'. It emphasized the importance of good governance in ensuring sustainable management of the natural resources and improved livelihoods. Chapter 2 underscored the importance of access to justice in the sustainable management of forest resources and improved livelihoods of the forest adjacent and dependent communities. It examined the adequacy of the law and practice in guaranteeing access to information in Uganda's forestry sector; examined the adequacy of the law and practice in protection and enjoyment of tenure rights of public forests adjacent communities; and the adequacy of the law and practice relating to liability for forestry harm.

It was established that although Uganda's forest law is generally strong, there are major gaps in practice that need to be addressed. Among the areas of strengths include the existence of explicit legal provisions providing for the right of access to information, provisions on the general procedure to be followed in accessing information and provisions on timeframe within which requests for information must be responded to. Uganda's forest legal framework also explicitly provides for specific offices in public bodies charged with the responsibility of ensuring public access to information. The major weaknesses of

Uganda's forestry legal framework are that it does not provide for any offence or punishment of public officials who blatantly refuse to respond to requests for information and it unnecessarily restricts the right of access to information to only Ugandan citizens. In practice, realisation and enjoyment of the right of access to information in Uganda's forestry sector is affected by lack of a manual of functions and index of records by the public forest bodies; general lack of up-to-date information by the public forest bodies; delays and non-response to requests for forest information; and at times blatant refusal by public officers to provide the requested information without any legal justification.

Chapter 2 further established that Uganda's forest legislation is generally weak with respect to the question of protection and enjoyment of tenure rights of forest adjacent and dependent communities. The only legally recognised and protected right is the right to cut and take dry wood or bamboo for personal domestic use. This right is moreover provided for in a very ambiguous manner which cannot guarantee its effective enjoyment. As is the case with the protection of tenure rights of forest adjacent and dependent communities, Uganda's forest legal framework is also weak with respect liability for forest harm. It does not criminalize many acts which are harmful or pose threats to forests. The penalties provided for commission of many forest crimes are also took weak in deterring forest crimes and illegalities. The law also gives a lot of discretion to judicial officers in determining the final sentences to impose once they convict someone for commission of a forest offence. Further, the law does not provide for any rewards to forest adjacent communities or other persons who assist law enforcement officers with information relevant on people who engage in commission of forest crimes and illegalities. Concerning redress mechanisms, it was found that Uganda's forest legal framework does not establish any forest-specific redress mechanism nor does it provide for alternative dispute settlement.

The chapter concluded by giving a number of recommendations that can help to enhance access to justice in Uganda's forestry sector. Key among these include: the need to introduce more forest crimes with respect to acts or omissions that have potential to cause harm to forests; the need to increase penalties for all forest crimes; the need to reduce the discretion of judicial officers with respect to the sentences to impose on persons convicted of forest crimes or illegalities; the need to provide rewards/incentives to persons who provide relevant information with respect to people who commit forest crimes and illegalities; and the need for the law to provide for more tenure rights for forest adjacent communities beyond the collection of dry wood. A number of recommendations were also made towards enhancing the role of courts in promoting forest justice. Key among these is the need for timeliness, judicial activism, and undue regard to technicalities in resolving forest-related disputes. The chapter also highlighted a number of non-legal challenges that need to be addressed to enhance access to justice in the forestry sector. These include the need to invest in: creating a manual of functions and index of records of public forest-mandated agencies; getting up-to-date forest information; and training staff of public agencies on the law and other issues related to access to justice.

In chapter 3, the authors presented evidence from Latin America intended to inform Uganda to prepare its citizenry to participate in the oil and gas sub-sector in a manner that enhances wealth creation and sustainable livelihoods. The chapter explored and highlighted some of the major limitations to local participation in Uganda. These include the fact that the majority of citizens and key local stakeholders do not have sufficient information on the investment opportunities in the oil and gas sector. This is worsened by the mindset of many citizens who think that the oil industry is complicated and requires a lot of capital; which is not necessarily the case.

The authors argue that effective local participation and benefit from the oil and gas industry is determined by deliberate government policies, strategies, legislations, contracts and actions that enhance the capacity of its citizens to take advantage of the opportunities presented by the industry. To this effect, the authors called for a participatory approach to development of local content policies, strategies programmes and legislation. It was emphasized that local content policy and strategies need to focus on: work force development; employment of local work force; training of local work force; investments in supplier development; developing supplies and services locally; and procuring supplies and services locally. Implementation of the local content policy should be guided by five key strategies: joint venture with local firms; training and skills development of local work force; developing local education and training institutions; industry collaboration; and improving local procurement by providing additional information, reducing the size and complexity of the scope, or simplifying procedures or processes to make it more likely that local firms will participate in the procurement process.

Once the local content policy is in place, it must be supported by a robust legislation that operationalizes the local content principles including creation of required institutional structures and allocation of roles. It is emphasized that contracts between IOCs and the government or sub-contractors should be detailed enough with specific local content requirements and clear responsibilities of each party. This is important to ensure actual implementation of local content provisions rather than depending on the good will of the IOCs through the corporate social responsibility principle.

Beyond the nature and scope of the local content policy and legislation, the chapter highlighted other important factors that influence the outcomes of local content. These include the ability to enforce the local content frameworks, the economic and social environment of the country, available technology, well-functioning national oil companies & monitoring Boards, and enterprise centers. The chapter also recommends that the Government of Uganda create incentives in the financial sector that promote local participation including providing soft loans to the upcoming enterprises to enable them participate in the oil industry.

Chapter 4 assessed conflict resolution mechanisms in the context of petroleum conflicts in Uganda's Abertine Graben. The chapter highlighted the number and nature of petroleum related conflicts in the Albertin Graben. These include unresolved communal conflicts, clashes between districts and central government, clashes between oil companies and government, conflicts between Bunyoro-Kitara kingdom and government and the potential boarder conflicts. It assessed whether the existing conflict mechanisms were robust enough to address petroleum conflicts and ensure enduring peace. It is emphasized that effective oil conflicts resolution requires the development, operationalization, and coordination of multilevel conflict-resolution mechanisms. It is argued that instituting prior conflict management measures before Uganda's oil and gas sector develops will make it easier to predict, detect, mitigate, de-escalate, and resolve oil and gas conflicts. The chapter emphasizes the need to tailor existing conflict-resolution mechanisms to oil and gas conflicts and stresses the need for bilateral and regional institutional frameworks to handle inter-state petroleum conflicts. The key recommendation for Uganda is to develop and implement a comprehensive petroleum conflict management strategy to prevent conflict escalation, avoid disruptions arising from lack of coordinated responses to conflicts, and resolve existing conflicts.

Chapter 5 was concerned with safeguarding community livelihoods in processes connected with land acquisition and expropriation for development purposes. Basing on three case studies, the authors argued land takings and uneven resettlement practices, often resulted in loss of community livelihoods. This was largely the result of loss of productive resources, having to survive on insufficient amounts of money given as compensation to replace income, and the absence of livelihood restoration programmes to assist project affected persons.

As argued, the existing policy and implementation for land acquisition in Uganda is uneven and inadequate for safeguarding the rights of PAPs. It was also established that there is a disconnect between the legal protection of the rights of individuals to land and livelihood as provided in policy and legislation, and the actual realisation of the rights in the course of implementing government development projects.

Development of a national "land acquisition, resettlement and rehabilitation policy" that "balances development" accounting for the needs of citizens, developers and industry and national Ugandan development priorities was recommended. It is argued that such a policy framework must be compliant with both Ugandan's legislation and international standards and best practices to safeguard impacted communities against social risks. To this effect, it was emphasized that "best practice" safeguards to avoid social and environmental risks need to be understood as a key component of the "cost" of any development project and land-taking. The authors also argue that implementing the policy would require building the capacity of institutions, project practitioners, and local governments to make good on implementation mechanisms that effectively reduce risks and improve the livelihood of impacted communities. They emphasize the need to fully engage project affected local communities from the start to finish, providing them with the entitlements, tools and guides that allow them resources to leverage the resettlement process on their behalf, in order to strengthen their livelihoods, food security, and social autonomy.

In Chapter 6, using Lake George in Uganda as a case study, the authors analyzed the fish product chain with a view of establishing why fishing communities in Uganda remain poor, in spite of having access to wealth in the fishery resource. It is argued that interventions seldom take cognisance of the nature, power and wealth relations over any resource as well as behavioral characteristics of main actors. As such, they have a dismal impact in terms of conservation and improving livelihoods. Using the analytical framework of nature, wealth and power, it was proved that a number of actors along the fish product chain act as mere conduits in whose hands wealth wealth passes, leaving no visible wealth impact to the local communities. Behaviour patterns among actors in the fish product chain also largely account for the dismal impact that the fish wealth had in fishing communities. For instance, it was established that while the *baria* and *deyi deyi* get some good money on a daily basis, they hardly save. They spend most of their money on alcohol and prostitutes. They believe and argue that there will always be constant income from the lake, and as such, it is unnecessary to save. It is recommended that policy makers and implementers should strive to balance a delicate and complex balance relationship between nature, wealth and power, if meaningful success is to be achieved in conserving the fish resource on one hand, and eradication poverty among fishing communities on the other.

Using experiences from Norway and Nigeria, Chapter 7 provided lessons for Uganda in ensuring that Uganda National Oil Company is managed according to best international practices. The authors argue that the Uganda National Oil Company can only play a significant role in the development of the country's oil and gas resources if it is well governed and managed in accordance with recognized standards and best good practices. Key among the best practices is that the National Oil Company must be run independently and in the interests of all stake holders. Appointment of the board members and top executives of Uganda National Oil Company by the President which exposes the company to patronage politics needs to stop. The chapter calls for setting up of competent and independent boards, establishment of functional internal and external audit systems and setting up of separate board committees to deal with matters of appointments, ethics, strategy and compensation among others. This is important for ensuring transparency and accountability.

In summation, from the different chapters in this book, six key themes stand out as critical for prudent natural resource management and sustainable livelihoods. First, access to justice is important, if natural resources are to benefit and improve livelihoods of the majority. Effective access to justice in natural resource management requires among other things: guarantees to ensure public access to information about natural resources; protection of tenure rights of resource adjacent communities; and effective redress mechanisms. Second, while development of local content frameworks are important for enhancing local content, development of a comprehensive local content strategy would be key to delivering benefits to the citizens. The strategy should combine development of policies, laws, institutional arrangements, skills-building and a robust monitoring framework with clear targets and time-lines to continuously assess steps and actions being taken. Third, realizing the full potential of natural resources in national development and improved livelihoods requires effective conflict prevention and resolution mechanisms that make it easy for the state and other actors to predict, detect, mitigate, and resolve conflicts in a timely, transparent and cost-effective manner. Fourth, the behavioural characteristics of natural resource dependent and adjacent communities affect the extent to which the wealth these communities get from the natural resources can be used to improve their welfare and livelihoods. For instance, it has been shown that for fishing communities in Uganda, while the fishermen earn some good money, they spend most of it on things less relevant to their welfare and livelihoods. Fifth, with the increased demand for land for national infrastructure development and investments, it is important that Governments in Africa develop legislative frameworks and mechanisms which while facilitating easy acquisition of land by Government, also adequately protects the rights of individuals including providing checks and balances to mitigate the negative effects on livelihoods.

Last, with particular respect to the management of oil and gas resources, the book has emphasised the importance of NOCs in generation of sustainable wealth for the country and citizens. For this to happen though, the NOCs must be run independently and operated in an efficient, transparent and accountable manner. The experiences presented in this book also demonstrate the need for Uganda to adopt local content frameworks including policies and laws in order to generate maximum benefits from extractive industries. This is important to increase local participation through increased skills and technology transfer, involvement of local companies and citizens and generation of jobs.

Improving governance of natural resources remains one of the most critical factors that need to be addressed to transform economies and livelihoods of the African people. Although the above-highlighted lessons and recommendations have emerged from analysis of Uganda's natural resource governance context, they are likely to be very relevant for other African countries as well.

Index

A

access to information, 27, 28, 29, 30, 31, 32, 33, 34, 35, 47, 48
Access to Information Act., 34
accountability, ix, 14, 18, 29, 32, 68, 69, 80, 117, 170, 171, 172, 180, 181
ACODE, iv, vi, vii, viii, xi, 32, 57, 61, 70, 100, 103, 106, 112, 113, 114, 120, 121, 130
Africa, vii, viii, 15, 22, 23, 24, 25, 56, 61, 63, 68, 69, 70, 73, 87, 92, 93, 94, 97, 102, 105, 121, 122, 123, 124, 127, 129, 155, 160, 164, 177, 182, 185
agricultural land, 21, 112
agriculture, 13, 16, 102
Albertine Graben, 13, 20, 75, 77, 78, 85, 91, 100, 114, 123
Albertine Rift, 78
alienation rights, 35
Angolanization, 60
arable land, 13, 14
artisanal miners, 13
Artisanal Processors, 136
assets, 15, 51, 83, 101, 105, 109, 111, 112, 115, 116

B

bamboo, 36, 37, 48
Beach Management Units (BMUs), 125, 137
benefit sharing, 15, 16, 17, 24, 129, 130
Benefit-Sharing, 23
biomass, 132
Boat Owners, 135
Buliisa, 79, 81
Bunyoro Local Oil Advocacy Group (BLOAG), 79
Bunyoro-Kitara, 79, 80, 81, 88, 91, 92

C

capabilities, 15, 53, 56, 64, 65, 90
carbon, 17
change impacts, 14
civil society, 15, 18, 53, 67, 80, 100, 105, 117, 118
civil society organisations, 19, 53, 80
climate, 13, 14, 17, 119, 131
Collaborative Forest Management, 37
communities, 16, 19, 21, 22, 27, 28, 29, 35, 36, 37, 38, 47, 48, 49, 63, 64, 68, 73, 77, 78, 80, 87, 100, 104, 106, 107, 110, 112, 113, 117, 118, 119, 120, 125, 126, 127, 130, 133, 134, 135, 137, 138, 140, 141, 142, 143, 144, 146, 151, 152, 153, 154, 155, 178
Community Engagement, 116
community forest, 36, 39
Community Livelihoods, 121
Compensation, 23, 25, 110, 111, 115, 124, 176
compensation procedures, 18, 119
compensations, 78, 79, 87
Conflicts, 73, 76, 78, 81, 83, 86, 93, 123
conservation, 16, 17, 19, 29, 103, 107, 119, 126, 127, 152, 153
conservation efforts, 17, 152
Convention of Biological Diversity, xi
corruption, 16, 53, 57, 69, 74, 85, 169, 173, 177, 178, 179, 180, 181
cultural changes, 17
cultural-traditional mechanisms, 90

D

decentralization, 15, 130
decision-making, 28, 29, 78, 84, 152
deforestation, 104
degradation, 13, 125, 135, 177
detection, 74

development, iv, vi, 14, 15, 16, 17, 18, 20, 21, 22, 28, 36, 51, 52, 53, 54, 55, 56, 58, 59, 60, 61, 62, 63, 64, 65, 67, 68, 75, 80, 82, 86, 90, 91, 99, 100, 101, 102, 103, 104, 105, 106, 107, 111, 113, 114, 115, 117, 118, 119, 120, 127, 151, 157, 158, 163, 165, 167, 178, 181, 185
Deyi-Deyi', 137
dislocation, 16
displacement, vi, 15, 21, 102, 103, 104, 115, 119, 120
District Forest Officer (DFO), 41
District Forest Officers, 33
districtisation, 85
diversification, 20, 51, 67, 69, 74
diversity, 15, 56, 131
donors, 19
dry wood, 36, 48

E

ecological, 16, 127
economic and social benefits, 16
economic and social transformation, 13
economic collapse, 73
economic growth, 14, 125
economic value, 39, 48, 125, 126, 153
economy, 52, 54, 60, 61, 63, 65, 67, 73, 75, 76, 77, 92, 125, 177
ecosystem services, 18
effectiveness, 15, 68, 86, 182
efficiency, 84, 174, 182
efficiency:, 15
encroachment, 40, 41, 42, 45, 46, 110
Enjoyment of Tenure Rights, 35
environmental democracy, 27, 28
environmental information, 28
environmental justice, 27, 28
environmental laws, 29
equity, 15, 18, 130
ethno-political mobilisation, 80
ethno-regional consciousness, 84
Evolution, 158, 183

exploitable natural resources, 15
exploitation, 15, 19, 20, 52, 60, 75, 76, 77, 78, 81, 82, 92, 125, 135, 141, 154
expropriations, 18, 119
extract, 17, 134, 166

F

fairness, 15, 81
financial capital, 15, 51
fish catches, 14, 134, 141
fish landing sites, 128, 131, 141, 150, 151
Fish Mongers, 136
fish processing industries, 14
fisher-folk, 22, 134, 142
fisheries, 13, 14, 19, 126, 130, 131, 137, 138, 142, 143, 150, 151, 152, 153, 154, 155
fishery, 22, 125, 126, 130, 132, 133, 139, 142, 143, 144, 146, 150, 153, 154
fishing, 16, 22, 116, 125, 126, 127, 129, 130, 133, 134, 135, 137, 138, 139, 140, 141, 142, 144, 145, 146, 147, 150, 151, 152, 153, 154, 155
fishing communities, 125, 142, 143, 144, 153
foraging, 16
forest cover, 14
forest crimes, 38, 39, 40, 46, 48
forest dispute, 27
forest governance, 14, 19
forest information, 19, 28, 30, 31, 32, 35, 47, 48
forest justice, 28, 32, 39, 40, 42, 44, 46, 47
forest management, 16, 17, 24, 29, 36
forest management plan, 36
forest produce, 39
forest reserve, 35, 36, 37, 38, 39, 40, 41, 42, 44, 45, 46
forest reserves, 33, 37, 38, 40, 45, 48
forest resources, 17, 29, 35, 44, 47

Forest Sector Support Department, xi, 31
forestry, 13, 19, 27, 28, 29, 34, 38, 47, 119
Forestry, xii, 13, 30, 31, 33, 34, 36, 37, 38, 39, 40, 49
fresh water bodies, 13
fuel wood (deadwood), 37

G

gas, 13, 14, 19, 20, 51, 52, 54, 55, 56, 57, 58, 59, 60, 61, 62, 64, 66, 67, 68, 69, 73, 74, 75, 78, 79, 80, 81, 82, 84, 85, 86, 87, 89, 90, 91, 92, 95, 100, 103, 104, 114, 158, 166, 173, 177, 180, 183, 184
GDP, xi, 13, 60, 74, 76, 101, 102, 125, 126
globalization, vi, 16, 22, 101, 103
good governance, 15, 127
Good resource governance, 14
governance, iv, vii, 13, 14, 15, 16, 17, 19, 22, 24, 25, 27, 28, 29, 32, 54, 63, 69, 73, 74, 78, 84, 86, 88, 90, 91, 92, 118, 119, 127, 153, 166, 169, 171, 172, 175, 176, 177, 178, 179, 181, 182, 184
governance infrastructure, 73
Government revenues, 82
Grievance Mechanism, 116

H

Hoima district, 79
human capita, 15
human capital, 133
human resources, 16
human rights standards, 28
humanity, 76

I

implementation, 15, 16, 17, 18, 20, 21, 30, 34, 53, 55, 58, 59, 60, 61, 62, 63, 65, 67, 68, 69, 90, 96, 100, 103, 106, 107, 112, 113, 116, 117, 120
implementation processes, 15

indigenous peoples, 14
industry driven interaction, 19
Industry Initiatives, 114
Information System Business Plan, 34
institutional change, 16, 53, 55
international best practices, 15, 113, 115
International Finance Corporation, 15, 17, 23, 100, 113, 114, 115, 116, 118, 122, 123
Interstate, 73
Intervention, 159, 163
Intra-state conflicts, 73, 78
investments, 17, 21, 53, 58, 64, 67, 79, 92, 101, 102, 103, 120, 125, 153

J

judicial remedies, 18

L

Lake George, 22, 126, 130, 131, 132, 133, 136, 138, 141, 142, 143, 144, 145, 146, 147, 149, 150, 151, 153, 154
land acquisition, 15, 18, 21, 79, 100, 102, 103, 104, 105, 106, 107, 108, 112, 114, 115, 119
Land Acquisition, 105, 108, 113, 121, 123, 124
Land Expropriation, 100, 105
land management, 15
Land Transfer, 100
landscapes, 17
law, ix, 18, 19, 27, 30, 31, 32, 35, 36, 38, 40, 44, 46, 47, 48, 53, 57, 58, 82, 83, 84, 87, 89, 100, 104, 108, 111, 113, 114, 115, 119, 158, 166, 167, 168, 169, 170, 171, 175, 178, 180, 181, 183
Legal and regulatory regimes, 18
Legal Framework, 17, 24
legislation, 15, 20, 30, 31, 32, 35, 36, 38, 39, 40, 47, 48, 56, 57, 59, 63, 68, 69, 100, 105, 114, 115, 118, 119, 125, 153, 185

legislative shift, 18, 119
liberalization, 77, 130, 159, 163
liberalization' \b \i, 101
livelihood, 13, 14, 15, 16, 19, 21, 29, 51, 54, 67, 78, 91, 99, 100, 102, 103, 105, 106, 108, 110, 111, 112, 114, 115, 116, 117, 118, 120, 131, 133, 138, 142, 144
Livelihood Restoration, 116
livelihoods, 13, 14, 15, 16, 19, 20, 21, 22, 23, 27, 51, 55, 79, 91, 100, 104, 105, 106, 108, 109, 110, 111, 115, 117, 120, 125, 127, 139, 152, 153
Livelihoods, 23, 25, 108, 122, 138
local communities, 14, 16, 17, 35, 36, 38, 41, 48, 79, 84, 99, 100, 102, 117, 120, 133
local content, iv, 15, 16, 19, 20, 51, 52, 53, 54, 55, 56, 57, 58, 59, 60, 61, 62, 63, 64, 65, 66, 68, 69, 104
Local Content, xi, 24, 51, 52, 68, 70, 71
Local Council (LC), 86
local government, 18, 19, 33, 82
local products, 16
local resilience, 16
lootability, 73, 76

M

mailo land, 42, 44, 45, 46
market growth, 17
marketization, 77
Matiri central forest reserve, 40, 41, 44, 46
Matiri central reserve, 42
Matiri Court Cases, 40
Matiri Natural Resource Users and Income Enhancement Association (MANRUIA), 37
middle income country, 13
militarizing, 78
minerals, 13, 16, 76, 101
mining sector, 13, 103

mismanagement, 74, 77, 85, 111, 178, 180, 183
Mukonomura, 41, 42, 44, 45, 46
multinationals, 77

N

national development, 13, 20, 21
national discourse, 27
National Forest Authority (NFA), 40
National Forestry Authority, xii, 31, 33, 34, 40
national revenues mix, 13
natural assets, 15
Natural Forest reserve, 44
natural justice, 87
natural resource governance, 14, 19
Natural Resource Governance, 14, 17, 23, 24, 70, 183
Natural Resources Governance, 71
non-complicity, 77
non-governmental organizations, 19

O

ocal content, 69
oil, 13, 14, 15, 19, 20, 25, 51, 52, 54, 55, 56, 57, 58, 59, 60, 61, 62, 64, 66, 67, 68, 69, 73, 74, 75, 76, 77, 78, 79, 80, 81, 82, 83, 84, 85, 86, 87, 88, 89, 90, 91, 92, 93, 94, 96, 99, 101, 103, 104, 107, 108, 109, 110, 113, 114, 119, 144, 146, 157, 158, 159, 160, 162, 163, 166, 167, 168, 169, 173, 174, 175, 177, 178, 180, 181, 182, 184, 185
oil conflicts, 20, 73, 84, 86, 89
Oil Sector, 86, 114
Omuhereza, 40, 41, 43, 44, 45, 46
operating licences, 13
operationalization, 21, 90

P

paradigms of policy, 15
participation, 15, 16, 17, 19, 20, 28, 29, 51, 52, 53, 55, 56, 57, 58, 59, 62, 63, 64,

65, 66, 67, 68, 69, 78, 79, 80, 105, 110, 116, 117, 130, 160, 167, 169, 174
Participatory Forest Management, xii
peace, 74, 87, 88, 90, 155
petroleum, 16, 21, 58, 60, 65, 73, 74, 75, 78, 79, 81, 82, 83, 84, 85, 89, 90, 91, 92, 103, 115, 157, 158, 159, 163, 165, 166, 167, 168, 169, 171, 173, 174, 176, 177, 178, 179, 180, 181, 182
petroleum resources, 157, 158, 163, 165, 166, 171, 173, 174, 177, 178, 181
petroleum-endowed economies, 74
physical capital, 15, 51
policies, 16, 17, 18, 20, 29, 52, 53, 54, 55, 56, 57, 59, 60, 62, 64, 65, 69, 101, 105, 106, 112, 113, 114, 119, 155, 171, 176
policy, vi, ix, 15, 17, 18, 19, 20, 21, 51, 52, 53, 55, 56, 57, 63, 64, 68, 69, 75, 76, 78, 80, 81, 83, 91, 92, 100, 103, 106, 107, 112, 113, 114, 118, 119, 120, 127, 152, 173
policy \b \i, 100
Policy Framework, 114
poor farming methods, 14
population, 13, 14, 64, 68, 89, 90, 103, 104, 112, 117, 130, 133, 134, 139, 142
poverty reduction, 14, 15, 22, 135, 143, 144
practical solutions, 15
prevention, 74, 75
principles, 14, 17, 64, 65, 81, 100, 112, 113, 172
private sector, 18, 53, 54, 58, 63, 64, 101, 102, 105, 117, 159, 162, 163, 168
Privatization, 162, 163, 185
production, 13, 22, 51, 53, 57, 77, 78, 80, 81, 82, 84, 89, 99, 102, 104, 109, 110, 116, 126, 130, 132, 139, 142, 149, 158, 159, 160, 165, 174, 177, 185
productivity, 16, 102, 130, 132, 133, 153, 168
property rights, 16, 18, 119

public forests
Forests, **15, 27**
purification of water, 127

R

raw materials, 16
reclamation, 134
Redress Mechanisms, 40
regulatory environment, 130
rehabilitation, 105, 115, 119
repackaging, 17
resettlement, vi, 15, 18, 21, 100, 103, 105, 106, 107, 108, 109, 110, 111, 113, 114, 115, 116, 117, 118, 119, 120, 123
Resettlement, xii, 23, 108, 113, 116, 117, 121, 123, 124
resettlement' \b \i, 113
resolution, 21, 22, 40, 45, 73, 74, 75, 84, 86, 88, 89, 90, 91, 92
resource wealth, 18
Responsible Governance, 18, 49, 118
restoration, 16, 109, 110, 112, 115, 116, 120, 164
revenue, ix, 17, 51, 78, 79, 81, 83, 84, 85, 89, 104, 127, 138, 143, 151, 152
Revenue Sharing, xii, 94
rights and responsibilities, 17
rivers, 13, 127, 131
rule of law, 18, 119
Rwamutonga, 79, 107, 109, 110, 112
Rwengabi, 79

S

security, viii, 14, 15, 19, 21, 29, 30, 66, 74, 77, 88, 94, 100, 102, 104, 106, 120, 154, 159, 171, 176
service delivery, 15, 117
service provision, 16, 18, 54
social capital, 15, 51
socioeconomic linkages, 73
sociopolitical configurations, 73
sociopolitical sophistication, 80

states, 19, 20, 36, 73, 74, 75, 76, 77, 79, 81, 88, 91, 101, 103, 157, 159, 160, 162
Sub-Saharan Afric, 24
Sub-Saharan Africa, 13, 25
sustainability, 15, 16, 23, 54, 81, 117, 122, 123, 124, 153, 154, 171, 176
Sustainable Forest Management, xii
sustainable livelihoods, 14, 16, 51, 52, 54, 157
Sustainable Livelihoods, 14, 15, 23
sustainable management, 14, 16, 19, 27, 44, 47

T

Tenure of Land, 18, 49, 118
tenure rights, 19, 27, 28, 35, 36, 37, 38, 47, 48
Tilapia, 133
tourism, 13, 15, 23, 67, 102
transformation, 17, 74, 77, 101, 126, 130, 173
transnational, 74, 77, 90, 92
transparency, ix, 15, 18, 29, 32, 53, 55, 69, 78, 80, 84, 115, 132, 169, 170, 172, 177, 180, 181

Transporters, 136
Traore, Karim, ii
Tullow Oil Uganda, 13
twin themes, 14

U

Uganda Human Rights Commission (UHRC), 80
Uganda Wildlife Authority, 131, 133
unemployment, 63, 73, 142
unprecedented loss, 13
urbanization, 85

V

valuable natural resources, 13, 105
value chain, 16, 60
vast arable land, 13
Voluntary Guidelines, 18, 49, 118
vulnerable communities, 29

W

wage-based income, 16
Weak resource governance, 13
wildlife, 13, 119, 127

www.ingramcontent.com/pod-product-compliance
Lightning Source LLC
Chambersburg PA
CBHW020948230426
43666CB00005B/218